FIXED

Dope sacks, dye packs, and the long welcome back

Dear Jocelyne,

hope you enjoy,
get well soon.

Best, Doug Piotter

By Doug Piotter

*I dedicate this book to
the still suffering addict,
and say, "Come on in,
the water's fine."*

My thanks to:

My lovely wife Terrell, who for years, was an audience of one before she had enough, saying, "you need a bigger audience," and shoved me out the door into the literary landscape.

My sentencing judge, the Honorable Carolyn Demmick, who had an idea that a lesser sentence would net lesser results before she hammered me.

My sisters and my late mother, for laughing at my stupid jokes.

My editor A. Scot Bolsinger, (effinartist.com) for helping me put together the Rubik's Cube that is my thoughts into something cohesive and legible.

Edie Everette, (everettecartons.com) for her wickedly imaginative illustrations.

The F.B.I. and S.P.D. officers, who I partnered with to solve all the crimes I committed.

My dog and cat and my recovery community, who said, "You should write a book" and have made it possible for me to live again.

My Dad, for providing me with loads of writing material.

Book One
Ill Will

Chapter 1

Bottom

I robbed my last bank on October 22, 1993, in Seattle, Washington. As usual, it was not a large take.

My dope dealer on that day was a female gangbanger chalk full of attitude. A thirty-year-old trapped inside a twelve-year-old body. Her street name was Lil' Bit. She showed up just in time to witness me push the launch button on the contents of my stomach, a trick I had been perfecting of late. Rendered speechless, she resurrected her childhood hopscotch technique to avoid my offerings.

I looked down at her and murmured, "I feel a little under the weather."

"No shit," she squealed with disdain.

Every fourth day or so, I forced myself to eat. It was a typical junkie's feast: half a convenience store burrito and a pint of Nestles' strawberry milk. I discovered through the process of elimination that these so-called food items were the only things I could keep down for more than a few minutes. My stomach immediately rejected anything else.

Retching had become like breathing, automatic. I did it all day long. Telltale nausea would swell into little more than the occasional spray of beer foam, my body's reaction to the steady stream of poison I injected, and smoked. I lived with an ever-present taste of bile and the feeling that I'd been swallowing broken glass, my new normal and all the more reason for me to want to medicate. Now and then it came up big, like this time when I painted the toes of her bouncing Doc Martens. *How's your attitude now,* I wondered?

"That's so fuckin' nasty," Lil' Bit said with conviction.

I waived off her proclamation, parked my self-esteem, and rallied.

"What are you doing later tonight?" I optimistically asked while I wiped the chunky dribble from my chin with my already dirty shirt sleeve.

"Getting my fuckin' money on, bitch," she answered.

I nodded in appreciation of her gangsta persona and made a mental note that the difficulties of her profession must have kept her on her toes. I paid her for the crack in fifty, hot-off-the-press two-dollar bills, all with consecutive serial numbers. This would have raised a red flag to any reputable merchant. She, on the other hand, didn't give a shit and accepted them.

"What the fuck you be doin' out there yo? I don't even wanna know," she said, thumbing through the lowly stack of bills before she passed the dope. With foreboding in her voice, she dropped a couple registers and said, "I been hearin' you ain't long for the streets."

I didn't care enough to argue, distracted with the task at hand. Dark days loomed.

I loaded up my glass straight-shooter, which had become an extension of my arm and put the flame to the yellow chunk of poisonous rock. I torched it until the wheel of the Bic lighter seared into my thumb, and the smell of burnt skin filled the air. The rock sizzled and disappeared into the stainless steel scouring pad, which fed me the smoke through the pipe. I felt no pain. My jaw moved up and down while I tried to access words but found none. A silent movie without the subtitles. My hands reached out for something wonderful that wasn't there. I had been trained to believe that this was love. I heard the train skid on the tracks as it arrived at the station inside my head. Then the floodgates of my sweat glands burst, drenching me all at once as my body temperature skyrocketed. My heartbeat became the pistons of the locomotive that was again on the move. I began to peel off my clothes as if I were on fire. I felt like I was suffocating and would choke to death. For about thirty seconds, I had never been so happy. All I could think about was more. This is what I lived for, over and over, a life unfulfilled.

Lil' Bit watched in rapt silence, then shook her head and said, "That shit don't look like no fun to me. Page me when you're out."

I nodded and accessed an "uh huh."

Then she laughed and said, "Fuckin' dope fiends," as she headed out the door.

The crack lasted about three hours. My freedom lasted four more days.

I had been holed up in a sleazy motel for a week, afraid to go outside. I had gotten into the groove of only coming out after dark unless it was to score dope or rob a bank. Each day, I had a goal worthy of every self-respecting junkie, which was to shoot a big enough hit of dope to get right on the edge of death, ears ringing, standing at the tunnel entrance—a common aspiration for the truly hardcore. The odds of going too far down the tunnel and not coming back at all were pretty good, sooner or later. I rolled the dice every day. I didn't want to die, but my will to live centered around the fear of missing out on that next big hit that would drag me even closer to the edge and unlock all the mysteries.

I grew beyond paranoid with my situation. I felt eyes were on me everywhere I went. I knew there was a $1,000 reward out for me posted in the newspaper by the local F.B.I. More and more people were getting wise to my shenanigans. Those who did know were weighing whether I was more valuable to them in jail or out. I enlisted a guy named Willy Nilly to cut my long thinning hair and dye it black. He learned the barber trade in prison. A coke fiend with scissors, not the smoothest cut. Even though the bank photos were crystal clear and obviously me, I felt that the haircut would add to my freedom, if only for a day. With itchy feet, the urge to keep on the move drove me.

Willy Nilly sold me a stolen van that I considered a steal for only $200. It came complete with a slew of empty heads previously attached to the shoulders of Seattle city parking meters. He had an apartment full of them, and the van was his overflow. He used the coins to feed his heroin meter. A nameless junkie also came with the van. Rather than vacate, the squatter invited me back to his family farm in North Dakota. He'd be on his way right after his stash ran out, or so he claimed. Of course he would; every junkie's big plans start after the stash runs out. Still, I leaned towards this idea. I thought a lot about a drive to North Dakota in my van with my faulty thinking cap and the take from the next bank robbery. I would become a farmer, a noble aspiration. Lost was the fact that snow would be the only thing covering the ground for the foreseeable future in North Dakota. This was late October, and I didn't even own a coat … or a snow shovel.

My thought processes weren't quite crystal clear.

I had other plans, too, competing for my attention. I entertained graduating to armed robbery. I had stashed a small pistol, a .25 caliber, so I was ready to roll, but the van I had bought was not. This van would only be good for a one-way trip back to my favorite crack house's driveway. A broken transmission line rendered all my fantasies meaningless. I always headed into the flames, never away. Drunk, I sat in the van for what seemed an eternity and willed it forward on to the next bank to no avail. Nothing I could think would make it shiny and new again, the only wheels that were spinning were the ones inside my head.

I used to say I had a $510 a day habit: $500 of dope plus $10 of the cheapest alcohol that money could buy when the dope ran out. That moment in the van was the $10 portion of my binge. The alcohol and the van conspired to render me immobile. My paranoia overwhelmed me. When I looked out the window, I swore that the ever present *THEY* were out there.

I holed up next in my partner-in-crime's Section 8 rental house and waited for something to happen. Billy Jibs, as I called him, had driven my getaway car in ten bank robberies. He considered it an easy gig, only slightly more dangerous than driving a taxi in New York City. He volunteered because he had two habits to feed, his and his junkie wife's. This was the end of a six-month binge, the trees had lost their leaves and I was tired. I had been like Insanity Claus on Christmas Eve to that house full of broken down junkies. They had been waiting for me to slide down the chimney with my big bag of dope and throw it around like it was inexhaustible. On this day, the stash and I were both exhausted. Nobody had a plan, and everyone was dope sick.

It's amazing to me how much energy, thought and effort a junkie will put into staying loaded and going nowhere. But for me the energy and effort were gone. The general concern of the others around me showed little interest in how I would survive, but rather how they were to get the next hit.

Billy Jibs, the neurotic New York transplant, a Woody Allen on smack, had a 5-year-old daughter, totally neglected, who lived with the daily graphics of a bustling shooting gallery in all its horror. She would tug on his sleeve while he had the end of a belt in his mouth and poked around trying to find a vein.

"Not now, Elizabeth," he said through clenched teeth. "Daddy's busy."

When the police showed up to save me from myself, they converged on the property suited up like Ninja Turtles, with helmets, shields, sticks and guns surrounding the house eight-men deep. Like Calgon bath oil beads had done for my Mother, the authorities did take me away.

Based on Willy Nilly's chummy relationship with the rescue rangers, he had not only sold me a van, he had sold me down the river as well.

I wasn't mad. My first thought was, *Thank God, what took you so long?*

"Let's go, Doug," they said, and I walked off to my new life.

Chapter 2
Not so Happy Days

As a kid, rebellion dogged my every step. I was on a trajectory, the snowball effect. It is only logical that minor incidents would gain traction, build upon themselves, cut a swath and carry me towards disaster.

I believe I was born when I was five years old because I have no recollection of my life before then. One of the first phrases I remember hearing was my mother's warning about "when your father gets home." It could have meant that we were going to eat, or it could have meant punishment depending on which way the wind blew. Those words would echo through my head for years to come. The anticipation was like watching the fuse on a stick of dynamite. I have since learned that not all kids were terrified of their fathers. Who knew?

William Sr. was a mythical creature who may have come home at 5:30 p.m., or Tuesday, or maybe not at all. I never personally got to know William Sr., a.k.a. Ill Will. He was a FINO—father in name only. Apparently his burden was a heavy one. He shut us all out and sought his comfort elsewhere. But he still left an indelible mark. Always the military man, my dad referred to us as his troops. Amused by his cleverness, he would lay down the law. Loudly.

We never had a conversation. This is not to say I didn't learn from Ill Will, who had plenty to say. He did all the talking—lecturing really—on the injustices of having to be an employee. I learned that anybody with money was "filthy stinkin' rich" and that was the worst. The proud, impoverished lifestyle we lived was a good thing in the mind of Ill Will. While I feigned interest, I would multi-task and drift off to someplace else hoping that I would someday become "filthy stinkin' rich", and despised by my father. My fantasies would have to sustain me until something stronger came along.

Ill Will was accountable to no one. He parented from long distance. This approach allowed him to escape the day-to-day responsibilities that my mother endured, yet still wield maximum authority. He chose jobs that required his absence most of the time. His ruse was that the big bucks he could make while away would lift us up and out of poverty. Unfortunately, for the rest of the family, the money never quite seemed to figure out how to get to where we lived. The combination of his blustery, alcohol-fueled communication style and the fact that he refused inquiries as to where his paycheck actually went, left the family shaking in our collective worn-out shoes.

Ill Will may have been absent a lot, but he was always around. He was a scary guy. His actions shouted loud and clear that he never wanted children. He ended up having five.

My brother Bill bided his time and made his escape when I was seven. He left me to deal with my harsh reality brotherless. I was none too pleased and filed away my displeasure to use against him at a later date in the form of petty theft.

My coping mechanism became a keenly developed style of sarcasm. I had a smart retort for everything said to me, which allowed me to take my lumps with some dignity. My complete escape would come about four years later when I discovered weed. Cheech and Chong were my heroes.

My big sister Vicki was delegated to the task of parenting. She was way more available, reliable and qualified than my father ever was. She did what needed to be done and for that I am eternally grateful. She umpired my little league games, got me off to school properly and tried to protect me, which was an unfair and overwhelming responsibility being a child herself. She was mature beyond her years.

Vicki had something to say though she often opted for other means of expression than words. She said it while she ironed her waist length hair. She said it with her straight-A report cards or her anti-establishment wardrobe choices. She said it to me with love. I worshiped her.

When both Bill and Vicki came out as gay at about the same time, Ill Will looked at me differently. He viewed me as his little hetero ally, us against them, his new number one son. Alas, to no avail, he would soon realize I was not on board, and again he considered me number two. He would have to keep on looking in the far reaches of Alaska, where he went in search of riches.

Stuck in bathrobe purgatory, my mom had no idea how to be a part of the great big world that existed on the other side of the front door. Life fed her a steady stream of sadness. She never showed too much joy or anger. Flat-lined, she held it all in. She was one hell of a poker player, which she put to good use in her golden years. She beat all the old ladies who lived in her building out of their hard earned nickels every single Saturday.

In 2012, when my mother was dying she told me that she had impulsively married my father in response to getting dumped by another guy. She didn't even know him. She had come from a solid middle-class background that wanted for nothing. My father had not. Perhaps, this explains why few family members talked to us, and even my parents didn't talk to each other very much. My father's preferred form of communication was by intercom, a system he had installed in every room of our rental shack. I thought it was pretty cool until I understood that he was a spy and could listen in on all the nice things his family was saying about him.

My parents showed no interest in my life. They didn't know what I liked or even the subjects I took in school. My mother existed in a fog of fear and anxiety, my father in a state of inebriation and rage. In that fog of their existence neither were able to meet the incessant needs of a child. They were absolutely unavailable. I became as un-needy and self-reliant as possible.

My siblings included in this order: Bill Jr., ten years older than me, Vicki, Pam and myself. Then there was Richard, who had come and gone long before me. I never knew there was a Richard until I was nineteen. I was snooping through my mom's personal belongings. She had a battleship gray steel lock box with no lock tucked away deep in her closet. It housed all the family secrets. That's where I found Richard's death certificate. I was so rocked by my discovery that I failed to look for any more secrets. All my siblings had known this minor detail but had failed to ever mention it. I had become the auxiliary replacement son. I wondered what else I didn't know about this secretive clan into which I was born.

The common suspicion was that Ill Will had been involved in a negligent way in ten-month-old Richard's death. He went absent without leave from the Navy for a year, which netted him a promotion and a raise when he got back. He left our mom's well-being in the care of her extended family. If there was ever any love in their marriage, it died right alongside Richard.

Ill Will's mother ran away from home when he was a young teen. This fueled his hatred of women. I believe my mother had so much shame around the death of her son and marrying my father that she stayed away from her family in Memphis.

How Ill Will stayed employed most of his life is a mystery. Maybe he had multiple personalities, intimidation, pity or lack of supervision. These are a few of the options I've thought about.

There was a time he and my brother had Seattle's largest morning paper route, five hundred-plus papers. As a young teenager, Bill did most of the work, which soon proved too much. The route ended shortly after it began. Bringing home the bacon wasn't one of Ill Will's strong suits, but eating it was. He was an imposing figure at six-foot, one-inch and 270.

Though Ill Will didn't take much to making money, he did scheme about it. He loved to spend time at blind auctions with the hope that hidden treasure would make everything right with the world. The fifteen or so broken down washing machines that ended up in the yard of our shack were, in theory, to be serviced and readied for market. Fast forward: under a thicket of blackberry brambles, fifteen broken down washing machines sat rusted and waiting for the flatbed Hearst to take them to the appliance graveyard.

The neighbors from Hell, no wonder I didn't have any friends.

Chapter 3

History Lesson

When my sister Vicki and I get together, the conversation eventually winds backward to the dark neighborhood of our childhood. I can't get enough. Being six years older than me she knows things, like what constitutes abuse. Showing up for kindergarten without a coat in winter, is that abuse? My memory hits a wall that she helps me to climb over as I methodically piece it back together in an attempt to have it make sense. Wish me luck.

Child Protective Services showed up at our door at the request of a teacher only to be effectively told to "piss off" by my father. Things were different then. I thought things were normal. The scope of my life experience told me that we lived normally, just like everyone else. Normal was sleeping on a table because there was only one bed. Normal meant appropriated military K-rations, fried baloney and cottage cheese for dinner. Normal often meant moving for one reason or another, adult reasons that required no explanation but served to land me in abnormal places like 23rd Avenue Northeast, the shack.

Not far away, South Lake Union is a high-rent, tech hub created by Seattle's favorite overgrown teenager Paul Allen. In the mid-1960s, it was home to the Coast and Geodetic Survey, my father's employer, and St. Vincent DePaul, the used everything store conveniently located right down the street. The second-hand store was an open-air grouping of scabbed together lean-to structures that seemed to go on forever. They looked slightly cartoonish, like a black and white photo of a Middle-Eastern flea market from a hundred years ago, a pall hung over the whole structure.

We would often get lugged around for a mandatory lowbrow family outing.

"Oh boy, we get to dig through someone else's discarded junk, again," we'd say later. But, at six years old it was my joy of living and the fact that someone died while wearing those shoes didn't matter.

"Who would pay department store prices when we can get it all here for practically free?" Ill Will would exercise his authority, daring anyone to answer.

We didn't answer but thought: "most of the rest of the developed world."

He asked my mother, "Babe, would you like a new pair of old shoes?"

He bought a pair of old boots for my mother, took his hunting knife and cut the toe to the sole and all the way around and made a pair of slippers that looked like they were right out of the middle ages.

Virginia wept.

William Sr. was a snappy dresser. Once he retired his military khakis for good, he fancied discarded lumberjack attire though he wouldn't have known which end of a chainsaw to use. Physical labor was for others more qualified.

He was a visionary and a Wranglers kind of guy. High-water denim jeans with suspenders to keep them afloat, a red and black thick wool shirt, lined and tuck-pointed with an over-the-top navy down vest, a black stocking cap rolled up twice exposing his humongous ear lobes. To pull it all together: sturdy, used slip-on leather Redwings. No matter the occasion, that is what he wore.

The first few times we went to St. Vinny's, it was kind of exciting, and according to my father, like a treasure hunt, which was his passion. The sheen wore off rather quickly. The rummage from St. Vincent de Paul helped furnish the shack. I was yet uninformed of Martha Stewart Living. My mother had read the writing on the wall. She started temping during Christmas at the Bon Marche` department store just to cover basic needs.

Chapter 4
Bingo

My parents used to take my sister Pam and me to the Enlisted Men's Club at the Sand Point Naval Air Station for some good old-fashioned gambling. My sister Vicki was twelve. She was also old enough to recognize Loserville when she saw it and opted out.

Pam was near perfect. She seemed to have avoided the shit end of the addiction stick that plagued me while growing up. She navigated all things little girl without any supervision—Brownies, Bluebirds, homework, and friendships—as she marched happily into adulthood. She was as close to normal as a Piotter could get. Sometimes I wonder if we really did live in the same environment, or if she was kidnaped and replaced by her doppelganger.

She did dabble in a little of this and that like any curious adolescent, but when the time came to cut it loose and turn the corner, she never hesitated and never looked back. Amazing. I wonder if my addiction affliction accelerated when she accidentally hit me dead between the eyes with a rock when I was four, or maybe when I hit myself over the head with an etch-a-sketch shortly after.

Her optimism has paid big dividends throughout her life. Always popular and very successful, she carved a straight and narrow path for herself leading with her magnetic charm and compassion in volumes. She's a gem.

In contrast, at age six, I was already a seasoned gambling spectator. Drinking Shirley Temples while watching adults lubricate and gamble was what excitement was all about. I had also experienced Long Acres horse racing track on a family outing. In keeping with my father's theme of all things Navy, we shared a giant submarine bologna sandwich while we watched our nag limp dead last across the finish line. We witnessed the wide range of gambler emotions and the verbal barrage Ill Will would toss about while he pissed away the family fortune. Ever the victim, he'd rant and rave and claim foul play. The possibility of going from rags to riches was a seductive elixir. It begged the question, "What were we going to do with all of that money?" The emotional swings and disappointment primed my pump for the day I could add some liquid forgetter and become my own alcoholic.

Six years old was apparently old enough to be in the dark and smoky cave of Multiple Vices even though my peers were curiously absent. Ill Will would keep me busy by tricking me into cleaning his pipes to shut me up and keep me occupied while he gambled. He made it seem like caring for his tobacco paraphernalia was an activity exclusive to special kids.

Bingo was an especially cutthroat business. According to my father, the odds were always in his favor. Losers were outraged and ordered doubles while vilifying the winners, and the winners were just a little too smug, doubling down on their cards for the next round of adrenaline. It was hard to see the blue hair through the haze of cigarette smoke.

As a retired Naval Squid, Ill Will appeared to have extra appendages while he played a countless number of cards, sliding their little windows closed and getting that much closer to Nirvana. As the clock ticked, he became a "more" type of a guy. More booze, more tobacco, more volume, more hand gestures, more language, more bingo cards, more embarrassments for me, but no more Shirley Temples. He buried himself in a mountain of spent pull-tab confetti. All in all, a successful evening, as far as Ill Will was concerned. A paycheck spent, a hangover coming, two bewildered, frightened children and a wife who wouldn't make a peep.

On the drive home from such excursions, the adrenaline wore off, and reality set in. A giant yellow sign would catch my attention. I saw it other times too, where it would glare at me from the top of my street on the way back from school every day. It hammered home a premonition of what I had to look forward to on my return. Not only did we live on a Dead End, but we were also at the bottom of a hill. Doubly cursed, things were bleak in the Piotter household. I remember it as the pariah house of hand-me-downs, the house of shame, nothing new under the sun. While the bingo halls, the racetracks, and the casinos stacked Ill Will's paychecks, the stuffing was coming out of the chairs in our house. Windows stayed cold and broken, covered with sheets that dripped nicotine. Multiple broken black and white T.V. sets stacked on top of each other created a pyramid that blared this or that game show through a snowstorm. The games shows gave my mother temporary hope that winning was a real possibility. White trash accouterment at its finest. This is where gray became my favorite color.

Chapter 5
Puppy Mill

Termite was our family dog when I was a kid, and I don't remember where she came from. Maybe she came with the hovel my parents had rented. She was appropriately named for masticating all things wood. On the plus side, she never devalued anything in our house because we already sat at less than zero when she arrived on the scene. It was my hope that she was practicing for the day she would shred the slumlord who often lurked in the shadows.

Termite was a Basenji mix, and she could chase cars at forty miles an hour. She was just as fast at having puppies. She never missed an opportunity, and she churned out litters twice a year. Our house always had that sweet smell of fresh puppies, K-9 after birth, and cigarettes, of course.

My mother was a game show fanatic, she respected and adored Bob Barker and would have followed his every command. Unfortunately, he would still be about a dozen years away from telling us, "and don't forget to get your pet spayed or neutered." My mother never considered getting

Termite spayed, possibly due to her Catholic upbringing. Mom considered it to be much easier for my sister and me to go door-to-door pushing pups.

"What kind of puppies are they?" the potential recipient asked.

"Them r dog puppies," I would reply.

It was an honest answer considering all the horny pre-leash-law male K-9s of unknown origins that trolled the neighborhood. Deadbeat dogs, all of them, and nary a one offered a stitch of puppy support.

No sooner would we have one batch distributed than the next troupe fell in right behind them. Termite was a well-oiled machine, very efficient. I finally lost count at thirty-five.

"Would you like another puppy," I would ask six months later.

Seeing as how there were only so many houses in that neighborhood, this was a legitimate question.

Once, I found Termite hitched to another dog while she faced the opposite direction. I tried to pull them apart to no avail. I ran into the house and found my mother.

"Mommy! Mommy! Termites stuck!" I yelled.

She shuffled outside with a cigarette dangling in her ever present bathrobe and custom-made slippers.

"Were gonna have some more puppies," she said.

It's the one and only birds-and-bees conversation either of my parents had with me. Mostly, I suspect, it was her way of conveying that I'd better start developing new puppy-marketing strategies.

Chapter 6
Virginia Slim

My parents weren't big on family photos when I was a child. But when I came across one, I was shocked to discover just how beautiful my mother had been. Life had taken its toll on her; she developed a hard edge thanks to my dad and me.

Virginia, my mother, was never much of a driver and with good reason. In 1964, she ended up on the short end of one of Ill Will's drunk-driving expeditions. With a broken nose, jaw and ribs, mouth wired shut and internally bleeding, she took her nourishment through a straw in the hospital bed.

A collective blanket of extraordinary shame covered my mom, my siblings and me when we saw the cars my father brought home. It was cruel and unusual punishment. He had a fondness for auction vehicles past their prime and all kinds of other faux treasures. Pay dirt was always just below the surface, or so he thought, after endless digging. That's probably why his fingernails were constantly in need of a deep cleaning. You would have thought the Little Orphan

Annie secret decoder rings he found inside the broken Singer treadle sewing machine were gold doubloons. Everything was going to be worth something someday.

Included in the parade of vehicles was the step van full of worthless galvanized plumbing parts. It was painted with silver colored roofing tar and a broom. There was the Renault that smoked so bad you couldn't even see that there was a car inside of that low traveling smog ball. There was the panel wagon with no radiator. He stocked it with about fifty single gallons of water in the back and pulled over every fifty feet or so to pour the H2O directly into the block. It was a very labor-intensive proposition and a real eye-catcher. My dad craved attention.

He was fond of guns as well and got me a B.B. pistol when I was eight. I immediately shot out all the lights in one of his prized clunkers and was charged with vehicular homicide. He took the gun away sentencing me to life without hope and a prodigious ass whoopin'.

My mom told me that the only new car they owned was when they were still slightly together.

My dad lost it.

When pressed about where he might have parked it, he replied, "Lost, as in poker game lost."

He was hard on cars and even harder on my mom.

It took Mom nearly two decades for her to drive again after the first accident and all the years of shame over Ill Will's automobiles. When she did venture back behind the wheel, she infused her courage with alcohol, thus racking up an impressive list of infractions just driving to the grocery store, bank and, unfortunately, the bar. A driving while intoxicated, a couple of fender benders and alcohol education class followed. Mom's solution was to start her own applied alcohol education classes that lasted until 2 a.m. most nights, becoming an "if you can't beat 'em, join 'em" alcoholic. This is a pattern she would adhere to for the next nine years before the end of her drinking. We would enjoy similar mother-son simultaneous meltdowns.

Still emotionally shaken from the effects of her accident with my father, Mom would be terrified when I would drive her around in her 1982 "we're the Ford Motor Company, and we've lost our way," four-cylinder Mustang.

"Ooh ooh ooh ooh," she would grunt as she tried to grab the wheel away from me.

She never fully adapted to driving. She just used increasing amounts of booze and cigarettes to stem the ever-present anxiety.

I grew up engulfed in cigarette smoke. In addition to Pall Malls, Virginia smoked More 100s, skinny cigar-type cigarettes. My dad smoked whatever you were smoking. If I hadn't spent as much time outside as a child, I'd probably be wheeling an oxygen tank around with me now.

At age 45, my mom was forced to work full time. Previously, she had worked as a seasonal part-time clerk to assure Christmas gifts for us. This was the result of my genius father's bright idea of quitting his high-paying job two weeks after the purchase of their first house. Ill Will would soon be gone for good. Prior to this, my mother rarely got out of her bathrobe. Totally checked out, I guess she didn't see the point.

On occasion, a pre-eco-friendly mixture of beauty supplies that would make my head spin more than signaled change was in the air. She sprayed and varnished and plucked and applied, squinting through one eye with a Pall Mall hanging out the side of her mouth. My big brother's bronze baby boots smoldered while chalk full-o-butts. I watched in horror while she tried to kill the persistent black patch that camped above her upper lip. She eventually claimed victory and ordered the Nair to stand down. As an eleven-year-old, I would have given anything for a Greek mustache like hers. Stuck in an aerosol-induced voyeuristic trance, I was fascinated with this production while she prepared for her double shift out on the town. She smacked her lips and hoisted her bra as an indication that she was ready.

"This can't be my mother," I thought to myself.

Mom would set out on foot for the three-quarter-mile trek down the old Bothell Hi-way to the Rimrock Steak House and Lounge. Like a long-running Broadway play, this discipline would go on for years.

One of my mother's pet peeves with me was the fact that my buddies and I ate up all her Ding Dongs and Ho Hos when we were high. Her grievance was justified. We mowed through them like locust. My mom was a shoe thrower, and she had plenty, not expensive or fancy, but damned if they didn't hurt just as bad when they stuck me in the forehead.

The bingo parlor where she worked was two bus rides and sixteen miles away from home, located in Columbia City, which at the time was one of the most dangerous parts of Seattle. She would work the noon to 10 p.m. shift four days a week for the next fifteen years until the days following an attempted robbery. A thief decided to jack her boss Clifford at gunpoint. The bingo parlor was huge and dealt in a lot of cash. So it makes sense to everyone but the would-be robber that Clifford would have a gun of his own. He shot the poor thieving bastard to death. Justice served? Clifford died shortly after completing his prison sentence for the shooting. The bingo parlor folded, as did that episode of my mother's life. Being uber stoic and tough as nails, she showed no fear and never complained, not even in death.

Being a 12-year-old with no parental supervision was akin to winning the lotto. Yippee! It was a long time before I realized what a sacrifice it was that my mother had made for me.

My mother was dealt a shitty hand and did the best she could with it. I loved her though it would take many years for me to be able to show her in a proper way. The day that Ill Will permanently vacated the homestead was the day Mom's seatbelt light went off, and she was free to move about the cabin. It was on. I too became free range at about that time, and we drifted apart. I would no longer be a Momma's boy, but soon would become Weed Boy, starting my lengthy party with a thousand forms of cannabis.

Years later, when Washington legalized marijuana, Seattle city officials sanctioned a smoke-a-thon under the Space Needle. The cops passed out bags of Doritos. I never thought I'd see the day. I had an extensive history with the illegal pot-smoking variety. Before I ever smoked weed, at eight years old, I smoked grass, literally, from a field. Dry straw rolled up in 8 x 11-inch lined notebook paper. It was a great way to internalize my homework. Smooooth. I had only recently started playing with matches with my little buddy Pete. The result was serious, smoking grass! We caught a field on fire. From then on, I laid low but Pyro Pete went on to burn down his house. This event caused me to take about a two-year little shithead sabbatical to reflect on my behavior, and I ultimately decided that I liked me just the way I was.

.

Chapter 7
Black Out

There's a story I often read about where whiskey is put in milk with the idea that it won't have an effect. My father used to put whiskey in his milk and share it with me. I know he thought it was cute me being five or six years old. Maybe this was his form of love in a bottle. As an alcoholic waiting to happen, it ended up being ugly for me. There is a photo of me at five years old tapping a keg of beer with my little friend. Today my little friend is in prison, a drug deal and shooting gone south. He's never getting out.

In the sixth grade, I had a friend who lived on the other side of the school playground fence. His mother drank fortified wine, which means we drank fortified wine, because, of course, we needed fortification. We helped ourselves. We would ditch bottles of Annie Green Springs, Bali Hai and Strawberry Hill on the playground. It tasted pretty good to me. I became an instant blackout drinker. There was no period of progression; it was already inside of me, as was the destructiveness that comes with such genetic coding. For example, one time at a party I crashed into a china cabinet, I never noticed the cigarettes that were put out on my face. A couple of years later I put the alcohol down for a time and only picked up weed. But I'd still swear I wasn't a drunk for years blocking out the blackout episodes. I could never successfully put alcohol into my system; it always ended up being a hunt for narcotics, followed by confusion and despair. Now, there is no more confusion about what would happen if I put alcohol into my system. I'm very clear what the outcome would be.

Weed fascinated me as much as booze flattened me. At eleven, I caught a first glimpse of my brother Bill's secret stash of Marijuana seeds. I was forever drawn to other people's stuff, so naturally, I was taken by his seeds.

Teach a man to grow and he can smoke for a lifetime. After helping myself to a free briar pipe at Market Time drug store, I loaded up a bowl full of the pilfered contraband seeds. I was unaware that seeds explode. It was like Orville Redenbacher's on the Fourth of July. I should have been wearing safety goggles. After my throat healed, and my headache went away, I began conducting my own scientific experiments. I quickly abandoned the seed smoking debacle and moved on to the stems section of the plant before working my way through the leaves up to the buds where I learned how to be a proper pothead.

The day I started smoking real weed, everything became clearer through the view of my red eyes. I took the position of that popular Doris Day song, "Que Sera Sera."

"Don't give a fuck a fuck, whatever will be will be." was my version.

I came to rely on weed for strength and to take me to a bearable place that didn't exist within my family. We were all planning our escapes in one form or fashion: my siblings and me through drugs, Mom by checking out, and Ill Will by running away. This worked for a long time until it didn't.

Weed rapidly became my best friend and constant companion. By the time I was eleven, I smoked it, sold it, grew it and played with it. I threw myself into developing new ways to smoke it and experimented with the latest in high-tech stoner gadgetry: bongs, roach clips, glass pipes, hookahs, power hitters, hot knives on a stove, soapstone, potatoes, gourds, bamboo, paper and fish pumps (sorry little fishies).

I even invented the Elephant Bong, my personal favorite, which resembled the trunk of the mighty Pachyderm. One person was like the pitcher and would put the lit end of a joint in their mouth and blow smoke through the end of a coat sleeve. The other person was the catcher in this analogy and put their head in the armpit of the coat to receive the smoke. My coats smelled like the inside of a bong, and yet I wondered how my teachers knew.

I've always liked to build things. As a teen, I was involved in a late night mission taking apart a plumbing supply shed. After leaving a heap of scrap metal and reconstructing it with my friends on the banks of Thornton Creek, a green space in the North Seattle neighborhood of Lake City, we had ourselves a serviceable clubhouse, including a nearby galvanized rain culvert that we used to sling kegs of beer down. This enhanced our eco-terrorism. The party was on. With thirty or forty junior alcoholics tearing up the eco-system, the neighbors were none too happy, but they never did a thing to discourage us.

We located our auxiliary clubhouse between the Midas Muffler shop's trapezoid-shaped, double-sided billboard on Lake City Way, the main local thoroughfare. We would smoke weed and have candlelight séances while raining fireworks down on the unsuspecting vehicles below. Our fascination with explosions and gasoline were prevalent.

My friend John's dad, Mr. B., would conduct gasoline bonfires in his backyard. We would cut up bowling balls with a machete and throw them on the fire. I don't know if Mr. B. was wrapped too tight, but to us, he was a hero. He had a Ford station wagon with a 390 engine in it. On the road, he used every cubic inch and drove like a bat out of Hell. We would pile in careening down the highway to this or that Washington State Park. Upon arrival the Jr. Reefer Madness Society would disperse into the woods and smoke as much weed as time would allow. Upon our return to Mr. B. and his Country Squire, he wondered if our eyeballs hadn't somehow come in contact with some poison ivy. He would beam proudly at providing us with such an awesome service.

Chapter 8
Father Knows Best—Or else

Before he left for good, Ill Will landed a real job in Alaska and a good one, too. Things were looking up. My parents bought a 1920s house with my own room where I could beat the shit out of my undeserving drum set. I looked forward to being a real member of a semi-normal family. The trade-off wouldn't be that bad: summers in Alaska with the family unit so my Dad could say, "looky here what I got," displaying us like zoo animals to his Moose Lodge buddies. Brother Bill would stay in Seattle and hold down the fort. It was doable, or so we all thought.

Ill Will's drinking and erratic behavior peeled out of the starting gate as soon as we arrived in Alaska leaving no doubt that the Cleavers had never existed. He taught me how to stand up straight and fuck off at the same time. We suffered from shame mightily that summer. The ferryboat ride back to Seattle was a magical adventure. That's where my mother had "The Affair" with the ship's purser. She was a sucker for a white uniform. While she had her night out, dinner, drinks, and dancing, we were all in her corner and cheered her on. She would repeat the big night two years later doubling her pleasure.

R.C.A., my Fathers employer, transferred him from Ketchikan to Nome, the equivalent of being Russian and ending up in Siberia. They couldn't fire him because he had the iron civil servant shield protecting him. We were ordered to follow our fearless leader north to Alaska and suffer together as a family. It seemed there were a lot of suffering families in Nome back then. We fit right in.

As a white kid in Nome, Alaska in the summer of 1972, I was quite popular with the Eskimo girls but not so with the boys. I got to experience prejudice from the receiving end. To add fuel to the fire Ill Will—while drinking at the royal order of Moose—would exclaim how I could kick the ass of any one of their "savage" sons. His brash claims proved very popular with the locals. *Thanks, Dad. Why don't you come down off your high and mighty barstool into the street and take this prodigious ass whipping you so generously manufactured for me?* I learned the fine art of curling up into a ball like a potato bug while getting the snot streamers beat out of me.

Menu planning became one of Ill Will's many self-proclaimed talents. He stocked plenty of Spam, Vienna sausages—which I like to think of as Son of Spam—Sailor Boy Pilot Bread, Denti Moore beef stew, Tang and indigestion for us to sink our grubby meat hooks into that summer. This fare was most likely the same shit he had been eating in the war. All of it had to be barged up from Seattle. I had already started smoking weed, so, man could I have used a barge load right about then.

The longest three months of my life came to an abrupt end when Mom put her foot down. Though an agnostic, she refused to live in that Godforsaken place one more day. My father's response was to make us choose sides. We proclaimed love for all-things-mother, forever hot-dip galvanizing his deep disappointment in us all.

About that time, my mother went to work. We were never closer. We were like partners in crime detoxing from Ill Will once and for all and living to tell about it. Although he was the one that did the ditching, it hurt a little less when I took ownership.

"I didn't want a father anyway," I told myself.

Now I could openly talk disparagingly about him, which made Mom laugh, confident I had a three-thousand-mile buffer zone that protected me from the open hand or the belt. Prior to that, he would ask me "how do you want it?" and I would say like it was no big deal, "Give me the belt." It was a minor victory and less personal, stealing some of his thunder.

Mom was very proud of the fact that she had saved up for a chest of drawers for me so I could lose the cardboard boxes. I think about that often. We spent a lot of time in the kitchen listening to Supersonics basketball games on the radio and talking about what life may have in store for us. It was a brief period where I garnered some attention from my mom before our dueling addictions kicked in, in earnest.

This was around the time Vicki, who was an exceptional student, wore bowling shoes and an army coat to school that said, "Fuck the Pigs" on the back. She expressed herself as anti-war and came out gay at an early age. Ill Will took special care in warning my sister Pam and me to steer clear of her for fear we would both become lesbians. Finding her coat quite fashionable, I wore it to Show and Tell to make my own statement. It was obvious from my fifth-grade teacher's reaction that she didn't think it a good idea to "fuck the pigs." It didn't go over well at all, like many of my ideas at the time.

One time, I pinched some weed from the Stepfather of one of my friends. I went out to brag it up. I had an invisible beacon on my head that said "come all ye stoners, let us break bud together." I found myself in the company of a group of older stoners who thought I was the cutest. My stock as a human being had seriously skyrocketed. I loved being a mascot.

A year later Ill Will quit his high paying job and moved back south to Ketchikan, Alaska, where he would be his own boss and not have to answer to anyone. He claimed it was a tax shelter because the I.R.S. dogged his every move. From that point on we would only see him when he was passed through Seattle on his way to a celebration where he was guest of honor in his own mind.

Chapter 9
Workin' It

Hard work has never been a problem for me. At age eleven, I delivered the morning paper. Up at four and to the paper shack, home by six. My account was small, only thirty-five papers, but it covered some serious acreage and had a lot of hills. I hated it but continued to suit up and show up even when tired, or it freaked me out. I just knew that this particular house on my route had the residential axe-murderer stationed behind the obscured glass door. I could see him sitting there waiting for me to let my guard down. To protect myself, I broke into another of my client's garage and stole a machete.

Just in case.

I daydreamed about doing battle on the street with this mystery killer while delivering papers. Soon my victorious mug would be plastered on the front page of the newspaper I tossed onto driveways. Just then I was bitten on the ankle by a giant dog, which snapped me out of it. It was about then I decided this paper delivery business was bullshit. I ditched my route on Christmas day. Merry Christmas you fuckers, no news is good news.

At Denny's that morning, I was treated to a 5 a.m. Christmas breakfast by one of the local creepy old pedophiles. I was never taught *not* to talk to strangers. I talked to as many as would listen. Who else was I going to talk to? I was hungry and knew that I could run fast, anything to avoid reality.

This was the same Denny's where my friends and I launched our Drano bombs, a combination of glass bottles, Drano, water and aluminum foil shrapnel secured with a screw top. We would slide these bombs down a tube that was sticking out of the ground. The fizz of the Drano would expand causing an explosion that would launch glass and metal fragments over the fence into the parking lot. After my meal, I went home to wait for the angry callers to inquire where the hell their papers were.

At thirteen, I got a weekend job washing pizza pans at Pioneer Square in downtown Seattle. Both my brother Bill and sister Pam worked there as well. As an added bonus, I sold a little weed on the premises making my $1.85 per hour look a little more attractive. This place was directly above Underground Seattle, a local tourist destination that was below street level and had remnants of Seattle before the Great Fire of 1889. The pizza joint had a door that connected underground. I soon took self-guided tours. Not a bad place to polish off that appropriated bottle of vino!

Being a working-man stoked my urge to drive. I felt I deserved to drive! And man did I want to take out the Red Sled. Even though my Mom didn't drive, she did own a 1964 Pontiac Grand Prix, a sleek, elegant, seductive car that seemed to go on forever. It talked to me continually while it was parked in the driveway. The needles of our two majestic fir trees that stood sentry at the entrance on the lookout for evildoers camouflaged the car, but I still knew it was there … tempting me. On this occasion, the mighty Douglas Firs made sure the Red Sled didn't make it out of the drive. At thirteen, I was not yet schooled in the art of driving backward. What I lacked in skill, I more than made up for in confidence. I put on my seatbelt, looked straight ahead, rammed it into reverse and stepped on the gas. I had reached my destination. The twelve or so feet I covered before I hit one of the trees and got stuck sideways, didn't take long at all to cover. Somebody had turned the front door to my house on its side. That motor had some juice. The driver side door was full of holes that were filled with sap. It smelled pretty good.

My neighbor Mike had just got his license and did know how to drive backward. After a few tries, he managed to rock it off of the tree and save my ass, for a fee of course. I may have skinned the tree, but my hide would be spared. My brother had it parked at the airport a week earlier so naturally someone must have hit it with a giant tree while it was parked there on the endless sea of concrete. My story had some cracks, and my brother wasn't buying it while he gave me the evil eye. I stuck to it until I finally came clean at age thirty-five.

Chapter 10
Jane Adams and the SPD

Jane Addams Jr. High School had a population of twenty-five hundred or thereabouts and it was the largest in Washington State. The school property was five city blocks long, across the street from Thornton Creek that ran parallel to the property.

With a school of this size, I saw a money making opportunity. My entrepreneurial spirit kicked in. If twenty percent of the student body bought joints from me every morning, I knew I could be shittin' in tall cotton. Me, Mr. Zig Zag, and my E.Z. Roll rolling machine went to work. Business turned out to be my best subject.

The motor pool was the school district's rent-a-cop agency, and they were charged with the task of busting up the morning smoke-outs and wrangle the little stoners back to class for their naps.

"It appeared that the creek was on fire," the motor pool's report would state.

The real cops often showed up for this or that problem. The Jane Addams Jr. High School neighborhood had become notorious for burglaries. The rogue student body knocked down houses as if they were bowling pins with stolen bowling balls in part to support their massive weed habits. Business was good.

One of the favorite student activities was to peel the Seattle Police Department stickers from the side of the cop cars and then re-attach them to the most studious students' lockers. This infuriated the police, but nary a word was spoken. We made it a "rat-free zone," which led to all sorts of interaction with the police. Though barely into puberty, someone had grown a mighty big set of junior balls and unbolted the cops flashing lights. As they drove away while responding to a call, the lights crashed to the ground. As incidents went, this was my personal favorite and a big hit with the rest of the adolescent-smart-ass-crowd.

By now I was a veteran of juvenile mayhem and I had a long list of credits that had transferred over from grade school. I was always on the lookout for likeminded individuals that could help me further develop my inner shit. A kid named J.P. fit the bill. He would later reach new depths and break the mold. J.P. was a muscular bundle of bad business, ready to leap with glee into the face of trouble that he manufactured around every corner. He was always up for a challenge. Do not enter meant come this way. He was magnetic, and a natural born leader loathed by mothers everywhere. I had no choice but to follow him.

J.P. had initiated a putty fight at Olympic Hills Elementary School by pulling all the putty out of the freshly glazed windows. Panes of glass gleefully fell to their shattering deaths one by one. This was hilarious to all who participated. J.P. was my kind of guy and remains my best friend to this day.

Jane Addams was a liberal school to be sure. For some added culture to arouse our daily doldrums, amongst other things, the male principal hired a belly dancer to perform in the auditorium for an assembly. Hooray! But for young Ken, the student evangelist, the thought of it was a touch too much. With the knowledge that the rest of us would all be going straight from the assembly hall to Hell, he tried to save himself by launching a protest that fell on deaf heathen ears. He obtained instant pariah status. And the show went on. It was a big hit.

During the show, the young evangelist showed up and acted like he was accidentally viewing his first porno movie. The sight of harem pants and jiggling human flesh appeared to contaminate him with the spirit of the devil, resulting in his wailing and gnashing of teeth. I don't know who was writhing more, he or the belly dancer.

Gambling for lunch money was another attractive vice that had become contagious. We flipped quarters odd or even. In its day, this was the equivalent of video poker, and for some, equally all-consuming.

Mr. Procter was our disheveled allergy ridden algebra teacher with that perpetual river of snot that flowed out of his oversized nose. Someone believed he needed a little help with the curriculum. He liked his coffee black. He got it black with an L.S.D. garnish. I tried to pay attention to his chalkboard presentation, which was quite fascinating, but I was distracted. His ever-present high water corduroy slacks were exposing the thick ropes of black hair on his legs, which via the L.S.D. took on a life of their own.

Kung Fu was the big show on television and L.S.D. was a big show at school. Many psychodelicised students threw metal fighting stars that they had fashioned in shop class. Come to find out this was a bad idea, but it did keep the school nurse hoppin'. Mr. Procter stumbled into a war zone as the stars and cartons of chocolate milk exploded onto the chalkboard. I could follow their trajectory as this algebra business was starting to make sense. The good teacher didn't make it past fourth period and excused himself and took some much needed personal leave time. Upon his return the next week his trousers had grown, his legs got a trim, and he appeared fairly well put together with his nose no longer running.

Nioki was a Japanese exchange student at Jane Addams. He was a brilliant mathematician and all-around genius with above-average English skills. There was a lot that went on inside his head. Not long after he joined the Doobie Brothers, there wasn't much of anything going on inside his head, but plenty went on outside of it. Nioki developed a voracious craving for weed and junk food. With both plentiful, he developed a mountain range of acne. Eventually, he blended right in with the Clearasil crowd and our cumulative C-minus average. He became one of us, and like me, he lived for weed. The folks back home in Japan would have their work cut out for them when he returned. They probably didn't have a lot of accolades for good old Jane Addams Jr. High. I hope things eventually cleared up for Nioki.

I was a real shit in junior high school. Those were my acting out years. If I were my son, I would have whipped my own ass, just like Ill Will had once done for me.

Chapter 11
Bugged Out

After a particularly strenuous session of picking psilocybin mushrooms, my cohorts and I decided to kick back and enjoy the fungus of our labors. There were trespassing signs everywhere, and 'shroomers were often confronted. We were doing our best to evade the red on the necks of the testy farmers whose property we were trespassing, These mushrooms, Liberty Caps to be specific, tasted the way dirty socks smell, but weren't too bad with a little Taco Bell hot sauce. Ebey Slough, a favorite among 'shroomers, is manure-laden pastureland thirty miles north of Seattle. It is loaded with the hallucinogenic fecal gold.

Like flies on shit, the 'shroomers swarmed over the bovine by-product. The competition for Liberty Caps and the pursuit of happiness was fierce. With an admirable bounty, we arrived back at my pal's rocket-sled muscle car, 383 cubic inches of Detroit's finest. We got in just as we sensed the 'shrooms were kicking in. Only then were we ready to roll.

As the thunderous engine started up, we were approached by a couple whose vehicle was in need of a tow. They looked vaguely familiar to me, possibly two of the countless stoners that passed through my weed convenience store, which also acted as a serviceable shelter for me, and my mother. This inconvenience had put a mild damper on the anticipated excitement of their maiden mushroom voyage. They felt relatively safe in asking us for a tow, but they were unaware that my pals and I had already entered an altered state. Good Samaritans that we were, we agreed to guide them home safely. After hooking their vehicle up with a rope and agreeing to let them off at the north end of the city, they piled into their VW Bug, and we were on our way.

Big mistake.

With the freeway signs flying by, creating kaleidoscopic patterns for our hyperaware appreciation, we noticed in the rearview mirror that there was a bug crawling right up our collective asses. The faster our Dodge Polara went, the faster the bug went. We would change lanes, the VW would change lanes. Try as we might, we couldn't shake it. I found this a little confusing because I had once owned one of these vehicles, and I knew that top speed for a Beetle was only about eighty miles per hour. Could the authorities have commissioned some new Anti-Shrooming Super Beetle? Or was it possibly an angry farmer who, had plenty of his own shit and was getting tired of ours? The folks in the VW had some mighty serious looks on their twisted faces. Surely there must be a way to lose them.

The plan we quickly cobbled together was to wipe bearing grease all over our faces and pull into the parking lot of the Woodland Park Zoo, jump out and disperse ourselves among the animals so we wouldn't be noticed. We were confident this would lose these feds or whatever undercover law enforcement agency drove super beetles these days. We realized that one of us might get caught and have to take one for the team. There were four of us and not one of us had an inkling who these people were. We made the thirty-mile trip back to Seattle in short order.

Screeching to a halt in the zoo's parking lot, we poured out of the Dodge. Then we spotted the umbilical cord of the VW. It all came back. A tow, oh yeah! In our misguided psychedelic attempt to throw our tail, we had overshot the Promised Land and dropped our victims off fifteen miles too late. They had been our hostages for thirty insane miles, burning up the brakes and steering like mad. The parking lot wasn't the only place that skid marks were laid down on that day. These two were in need of fresh laundry. The bugged out bug owners declined our heartfelt offer for a tow back the other way and decided to call AAA.

Chapter 12
Hats Off to Shepp

I thought my dad was a bad actor—and he was—but eventually he was my dad only from long distance. Add to this a wide variety of narcotics both natural and manmade that I used and our relationship became easier to navigate. On the other hand, my friend Loren's stepdad was around 100 percent of the time. To call him brutal would be an understatement. Ill Will looked like a scout leader by comparison. No wonder Loren was the first of my friends to get sober.

Everyone in the neighborhood knew there were five wild dogs living in Loren's back yard. You wouldn't think that Golden Labs would fall under that category, but these dogs were made to be crazy. They weighed in at about one hundred pounds each. Shepp was their pack leader. To show his love for these animals, Loren's stepfather would beat them with a stick and make them fight over the food. That's just about what went on inside the house as well.

Next door to Loren was Big Dave's, a known haven for all things weed. Loren didn't have to go far to find relief. Like me, Dave sold drugs out of his mother's house.

On this day, sleazy Greg slithered out of his car with a seal-a-meal package full of weed. Greg was a lowbrow dealer who had infiltrated my sphere of homeboys. In addition to misting his weed with a spray bottle for added weight, he gouged prices when supplies ran low. He was about as popular as genital warts, but our collective weed habit dictated our tolerance level for him. Never careful to not create a scene, Greg parked on the upper level and left his motor running and the door open to his smoking eyesore. Some well-intended neighbors took this to mean that there was a burglary in progress. They called the cops and then they called Dave. With the news that the cops were en route, Greg beat feet out the lower level back door with his bag o' buds in tow.

Those dogs may have been mean, but they were not stupid. They knew how to be quiet if they sensed an unsuspecting meal had just fallen off the turnip truck. Unaware of the stealth man-eaters, Greg's logical escape route was to hop the fence into the neighboring backyard, circle around the front to his car and get on down the road. That plan was a bust when Shepp and company attacked.

The police heard the commotion. They bounded over the fence and gave chase. It sounded like a wildebeest being shredded by a pack of hyenas on the Serengeti.

Greg barely made it out, but the coveted weed did not. Now these dogs would have the munchies. Too bad he didn't drop some Twinkies and chocolate milk as well. The cops also barely made it out. One of their hats did not. There was a wire rim, a badge, blue fabric and green buds strewn all over the yard. After sending Loren in for reconnaissance, we discovered that the buds were a total loss, being mixed in with animal feces and all.

The fiasco was written off as a false alarm by the policemen in black and blue and a warning sign for Sleazy Greg to shed his skin elsewhere. There was no blowback, so it was business as usual. We saw neither in that neighborhood again. As for Shepp, Loren, and company, they went back to their steady diet of abuse.

Book Two
Blunder Years

Chapter 13

The Iso

Aside from the ever-present stash of girlie magazines, most mid-1970s teenage boys read *Popular Mechanics, Boys Life* or some other educational rag with middle-of-the-road redeeming qualities. My higher education came in the form of *High Times* magazine, which has no redeeming qualities. I, of course, loved it. I even bought clothing out of *High Times*, generally, T-shirts with pictures of buds from around the world. Good to smoke and good for a geography lesson.

When I saw the colored illustration and description of a new unbelievable gadget, I knew I must have this money-making machine called the Isomerizer. It would be my goose that laid the golden eggs. To a non-stoner type person, it could be used to make different varieties of essential oils, like lavender, that you dab behind your ears. I had my own version of *essential* oil. My oil was best when smoked in a glass pipe.

You could take the undesirable worthless leaves off of even a lazy male marijuana plant and watch its glorious transformation into vats of amber T.H.C.-laden honey oil. Cha ching, truly, my manna from *High Times* heaven.

I chose the Iso 2 for $159. It came complete with a compartment to cram the leaves into, what looked like a transmitting station on top, and a small catch basin or oil pan. The unit was all-inclusive, eliminating the need for glass decanters, a complicated lab and possible explosion due to the isopropyl alcohol, heat and the education level of the chemist. Drug manufacturing for dummies.

After leeching the oils out of the plant material and running it through as many as three times to create a sticky amber liquid, my own Mary Jane Oil was ready for market, though not much made it that far. I was my own best client. I would cough and cough and cough some more as I tested the limits of the human lung until I couldn't breathe and thought my head would explode. Then I would do it again.

Yeah, man.

I learned valuable life skills in my personal science lab, inside my bedroom in my mom's house.

I cultivated my clientele and carried them with me across the street from Jane Addams Jr. High to Nathan Hale High School. One of my favorite activities besides smoking weed was swimming. It gave me a reason to have red eyes all day at school. I became a very good swimmer. In high school, I also excelled at drama because it gave me a chance to be someone else for a change. That was something I had always longed for.

Fridays in drama class were improvisational skit day. Determined to improvise well, we often get high and went out in search of material. It was a good excuse anyway. There was nothing like a Tangerine Dream concert on acid to get the creative juices flowing. In their day, Tangerine

Dream, five German guys that played synthesizers, was the psychedelic band of choice. They looked more like scientists in lab coats that twisted knobs than musicians that played instruments. The only reason we realized the concert was over once we snapped out of Wonderland was because of the brutal flickering overhead lights and the fact that the roadies had finished moving most of the equipment off the stage of the Paramount Theater.

We all piled back into J.P.'s Studebaker Lark to head back to the school parking lot and practice our new-found material for our improv show the next day. Due to a mechanical malfunction in the Lark, top speed in this baby was 25 mph., any faster and the steering column would shake so violently it was just like re-entering orbit in a spacecraft. If anyone could make this jalopy go faster, it was John Patrick. He lived to push things to their absolute limits. J.P. squeezed the wheel so hard it looked to me like his knuckles would explode. On the freeway with cars whizzing past at an incredible 55, we discovered yet another problem. It was raining in sheets and blankets, and the windshield wipers could only be controlled by jerking the steering wheel from twelve to three o'clock. The far right lane was the place to be as we mimicked a game of chicken with the other drivers; we veered toward them through the rain only to pull back abruptly. Unnerved, J.P. was definitely in his zone. That was a nice cherry on top of our acid trip. We spent the evening coming up with all kinds of hilarious ideas for our Friday skit. We knew we'd kill it. Unfortunately, the next day the hilarious ideas were well past their due date unless we were willing to give out acid to the entire school audience well in advance so they could appreciate just how hilarious we were the night before.

"Good judgment comes from experience, and experience comes from bad judgment," Rita Mae Brown would say. It might as well have been my life's theme song. It was never my intention to be so out of control. I longed for a so-called, normal life with parents who knew me and would help me develop some dreams. Instead, I had no dreams. My childhood had set me on a path of experiences that lacked sound judgment while I built a dream state through chemistry. It brings to mind a saying that goes like this: "People generally go in the direction that they're headed." That was certainly true for me. I was already going down, down, down.

Chapter 14
The Reverend

The Reverend resided directly behind me. He had gone to a Catholic parochial school before transferring. The nuns failed miserably. But it's hard to blame them much if you knew the Reverend. It would have been like trying to make a pet out of a Coyote. He believed in his own sacred text and proved to be untamable. The threat of nun-chucks wasn't enough of a deterrent to make him genuflect. He stayed true to his calling. Finally, they repented and released him back into the wild of Nathan Hale High School. We quickly adopted him as one of our own.

Many of my friends were either adopted or still residing with parents who wished they had opted for adoption. This created a nearly unbreakable bond, the Bondo brothers. Ignorant of the ins and outs of the religion industry, my Heathen High School homeboys and I didn't know that being Catholic would have made him The Father. That would have been weird, so we dubbed him The Reverend. He had a "take what you like and leave the rest" attitude when it came to religious offerings, reciting the occasional

Bible verse while smoking a more-than-occasional joint. The Reverend was a mysterious Mediterranean looking kid, with curly black hair, olive skin and piercing green eyes. He ran faster in flip-flops and trench coat than any one of Nathan Hale's heralded jocks from the track team. He could fly high enough to stuff a basketball. Being shamed by a stoner really pissed them off.

It was agreed that The Reverend honed his fleet footedness while evading the gang of ruthless nuns at Saint Mathew's Parochial School.

No one ever actually saw The Reverend's adopted parents or had been inside his house. At times, I did see him lean out of the window over his garage and assess the situation below.

The Reverend had the longest hair in school, black and curly, waist length. He was a quiet skinny guy, often ruminating and occasionally telling one of us "shut it, Dummer" through the side of his mouth, like a gangster. Though economic with his words, you could look through his hair and see the intellectual wheels constantly churning inside his head. He had his own language and spoke in Snoop Dog English when Snoop Dog was just a pup. Shznit mzan, he knew things. There were rumors that he had done heroin with the hardcore Catholic kids. People gravitated towards him.

I started attending Catholic Church on a weekly basis at the Reverend's urging. Well, that's not entirely correct. I started attending the parking lot of the church's school at night to be more specific, where its fleet of buses was stored. The Reverend called this his personal self-service filling station.

"Forgive me, Father, for I have siphoned," I'd say after sucking gas through a hose.

The Rev shared his personal fleet of Catholic school buses with me, each of which held a heavenly amount of gas. We depleted them on a rotation to spread the love and remain anonymous. We went forth with full tanks of our own and continued to do good works. The Reverend figured it was a way for us to help them give back to their community. I was glad I could be of service.

Chapter 15

Downhill Racer

The question plagued me.

"Why was I the one to always get arrested?"

Everyone seemed to know the answer but me. I would have plenty of time to work on this mystery puzzle locked up in the Bothell City Jail.

Our plan was to skip school, pile into Kagi's van and hit the slopes for some night skiing, but the adventure had gone south fast. On an impulse, my buddy J.P. went into a liquor store in his ski gear, which included goggles with the intention of buying alcohol. He was just a tad conspicuous. Being just 17 years old he was four years shy of legal but figured he'd give it a shot. He failed to mention his plan B. I should have known it would be adventurous with J.P. involved. Not two weeks earlier on the way up, the hood of J.P's. car detached and flew backward over the top of the car and crashed on down the mountainside as we motored along at ninety miles per hour.

He didn't slow down or blink and said, "Don't worry, it'll be good, let the motor breathe" as he pitched a beer can on out the window.

I wasn't reassured.

Drama with J.P. was a given. Refusing to be denied the booze he wanted, J.P. returned to the van with a half-gallon of something amber under his ski parka that was 100 proof and most likely made from nutritious grain. We then filled the empty gas tank and headed out with the goal of hitting the slopes before fourth period started.

Back on the road, our excitement brewed. We stoked and smoked our bowls and passed the stolen bottle around. That's when we noticed the red and blue lights coming up fast. Only then did J.P. mention that he didn't purchase the booze with his goggles on. He helped himself in the liquor store with his face showing. We knew we were obviously all going to jail as we pulled over.

One by one we were brought from the van to the patrol car to rat on one another for the crime committed. One by one we declared that no one knew a gosh-darn thing. As it turned out, we didn't know a thing. In the midst of our giant adrenaline rush from J.Ps. booze caper, we had forgotten to pay for the gas.

The cop bought our story and escorted us back to the gas station to pay our tab.

He then looked over our group and said, "You're free to go," until he looked at me.

"Not you," he said.

I waved goodbye to my warrant-free friends from the back of the patrol car with my hankie as it pulled out to take me to jail. Seems I had a something or other that I hadn't quite dealt with court-wise. Priors, we call 'em. I had already been in juvenile detention as well as the Wallingford police station lockup in Seattle proper. I fully expected my accomplices to leave me to rot and die in this suburban redneck jail while they partied on the slopes. Loyal that they were, they went back to the parking lot of Nathan Hale High School, took up a collection and came back to bail me out. We managed to start the process all over again and ski the night shift.

This was about the time when music ruled my brain waves as much as getting high and wreaking havoc. I went to just about every rock concert in Seattle from 1972 to 1978, whether I liked the band or not. Kiss was one band that I got into for free. It was so disappointing I wanted a refund. I hoped to see those clowns catch themselves on fire with their worn-out pyro routine and pornographic tongues, alas, to no avail.

A friend of a friend worked the door of the then Seattle Center Coliseum (currently Key Arena and home of the Seattle Storm women's basketball team and former home of the Oklahoma City Sonics.) He would let groups of us in for free. When he couldn't get us in, rushing the doors was the next best choice. Inevitably, someone got caught in the melee. Sometimes the person caught would be me. We continued to hunt for a better plan.

A friend and I were industrious and fairly artistic, so we started making tickets. My honed business instincts kicked in as our ticket-making venture proved to be profitable. Cheap counterfeit tickets were in high demand.

We used multi-colored laminated paper, a Smith Corona typewriter with no ink to make the indentations, appropriate colored fingernail polish painted in the indentations, pen and ink and a little luck and a lot of drugs. Voila! In those days, tickets were not so sophisticated, obviously. We factored a combination of heavy crowds and distracted ticket-takers into our success plans. The Stones, Joe Walsh, and Led

Zeppelin were a few of the concerts I successfully entered. Turns out I didn't need my Zeppelin counterfeits after all when I was pushed by the crowd right through the shattered glass doors. I hope they don't take me back and try me as a juvenile, even today.

Chapter 16

Graduation

Smoking weed stopped being a looked-forward-to event and became an as-necessary-as-insulin-for-a-diabetic event. My anxiety over having enough weed, to chill me out, was as thick as the smoke haze around me.

Needing weed meant an always-stressful, never-ending hunt for a supply source. There was the anxiety of possessing weed and the anxiety of not possessing it. There was my inability to accomplish anything useful while smoking it, and the shame that came with not being productive, being dumbed down. I also stressed about compulsive eating. Then there was the fear that this was my life, that I had peaked as a person and was an undesirable. An open wound with nothing to contribute. With all that guilt and paranoia, it felt like I had a dark character from a Freak Brothers underground comic book occupying space inside my body.

My graduation to narcotics soon followed. Once I got a taste, that was it. It would be like that Willie Nelson song, "You Were Always on My Mind." Cocaine instantly spun me out. It would be my main focus for the next fifteen years.

All my jobs were just clunker vehicles that carried me to my next binge. Genius that I was, I thought I could be bigger than that little white powder.

I replaced the word "weed" with "cocaine" in everything I once did. Whatever it took to get my hands, nose, arms and lungs on cocaine would be my mission. I fell into a pit of moral decay and hit the bottom rungs of society. The day would come when there was nobody left for me to look down on, no one that I could look to and comfort myself with the fallacy *I'd never be that bad*. I was it. I had reached the bottom, and I kept right on digging—until the Feds took away my shovel.

Coke wasn't my only addiction. I considered Deanne a blue ribbon prize. I won her over with my big bag of blow and bottle of Chivas during an all-nighter when I was seventeen and the center of the universe. She was a bright and shiny object of my affection to be added to my collection. She was exotic, of Asian descent. In my mind, she was a diamond. In reality, a cubic zirconia. I wanted to show her off wherever I went. I would be the envy of all my friends. My social currency was on the rise.

An ultra-conservative Christian couple adopted her at the age of 12 and loved her just because. They provided her with food, shelter, and the good book. It proved inadequate. She had her sights set lower. She was street-wise and hardened beyond her years, a person of few words but always smiling her calculated toxic smile, which said, you're fucked. Already a veteran runaway at fifteen, she put her parents through their paces.

I assured her parents I'd have her home by 10:30 p.m., I just didn't say what day.

"I'll do whatever the fuck I want, and come home whenever I want," Deanne said.

I cringed.

Locking her in her room was a tactic that didn't net their desired results. She broke the door down, then broke their hearts.

I bribed her with drugs and money and expected her to be in lock step with my desires. I would have unlimited access to her body. Anything more than utter disappointment could never have been achieved under the circumstances. She had her own agenda. My moral compass was still a couple of decades away from the right direction.

This arrangement worked for a time, but there were limits to my magnetism. She had a habit of disappearing on me and not talking about it. I had no supervision of my own and did the same thing, but my double standard didn't bother me.

When pressed, she said, "What are you, my new Dad?"

She could have stuck a knife in me, and it would have stung less. She looked at me as if I was just another authority figure who told her what to do. I wanted to be her everything, but I was no better than a john. Though I would learn to dislike her personally, I felt a need to have her, no matter the cost. I chased the unavailable. Deanne temporarily wanted what I had, and she got it. We never discussed beyond temporary.

"I'm pregnant," she said to me as if she had said, "I'm hungry."

Abortion was an easy decision. Both of us were still children ourselves, so we decided babies didn't need more babies.

I thought that going through something like an abortion meant that we were thick as thieves. Deanne thought not. She liked me less each day.

"I'm the one who had to straddle the fuckin' stirrups, not you," she said and began to pull away from me in earnest.

Soon a nearby neighborhood gang claimed ownership of her. Deanne offered no objection. She took flight easily in any direction and ran away with a boy named Phil. She didn't come back to me, but Phil did soon enough, along with his tribe, who visited my mother's house to take me down.

She had been groomed and told them everything she knew about me.

Phil introduced himself by kicking in my front door. Five crazed assholes entered my personal space. One stuck a gun in my face.

"Where's the fuckin' dope?" Phil yelled.

"I don…" I stammered.

"Shut the fuck up or I'll gut you," said a thug named Lo, as he waved his impressive Bowie knife. As if the gun wasn't threatening enough.

"On your knees," one of the clones said.

He duct-taped my mouth and tied me up.

They shoved me face down. I could only hear the damage as they went through the house like wrecking balls. They pulled the phone out of the wall, cut holes in my beloved set of Ludwig drum skins and tossed my mom's room looking for jewelry or anything else of value. They took a few things and some money, but never found my stash.

They were not stoked about that.

The time ticked so rather than coerce the location of my stash, they got gone, leaving me bound and sick over the knowledge of Deanne's betrayal. As treasonous an act it was, I still couldn't get her out of my sick head, pure poison.

My neighbor friend Gary had observed the action in real time. Once the goons left, he came over to help me put things back together.

"I'll go call Kevin, he works for Ma Bell," he said.

An hour later the phone was fixed. I'm sure my mother was afraid because she pretended not to notice and suffered in silence. I never mentioned it to her for two more decades.

I decided Deanne and I could patch things up, forgive and forget. Soon enough we did get back together briefly but only until the sequel of our drama *Home Invasion 2*. She and Phil and the goons repeated their visit and trashing of my home. My mom repeated her silence. The only thing that didn't repeat was my addictive pursuit of Deanne. I stuck to the coke.

About a year into my cocaine test study things were getting a little unpredictable. Against all council, I dropped out of high school with one credit to go. This prompted my mother to abruptly kick me out of her house. She was maxed out by all the regular visits from the Seattle narcotics squad and the gangs of thugs that kept tying me up and robbing me at gunpoint. I don't know which byproduct of my drug dealing was worse with both groups busting up the house in excess. My Get Out Of Jail Free card had long expired and the seclusion and familiarity of my mother's house that had kept me off the police radar for a number of years expired along with it.

Chapter 17

Turtle Dick

Now out on my own, I sought to regain a cloak of invisibility. I moved into a house in Seattle's University District with my big bag of weed right next to a high-rise senior living facility. What would cops want with a senior citizen home, I reasoned?

To my surprise, my comings and goings were well documented by the eagle eye retirees and post haste I was busted again, acquiring another felony. Lo and behold, Ill Will swooped in right on cue, to show off his stellar parenting skills.

Both Ill Will and I thought I could've just parked my addiction at the Greyhound terminal, miraculously become drug-free and live happily ever after. We were both very wrong.

He tried to farm me out to his younger brother in Maine whom I had met for about two hours when I was fifteen. The gist of my uncle's response went like this: "I'm not adopting any eighteen-year-old drug addicts right now Bill."

I was crushed because I was slightly insane. It seemed like the logical thing to do.

Oh, how I had longed to be wanted one day.

So we went to Plan B. I had an abundance of plan Bs. I'd go make a bunch of money on a fishing boat. That'll cure me. I followed my sick father to Craig, Alaska and got a job with Turtle Dick, not a commentary on what was under his manhood, but rather alluding to the fact that he had once shot a 150-year-old, 1,300-pound Japanese sea turtle. He almost lost his fishing license and got a big fine from Alaska Fish and Game.

Turtle Dick, my dad's best friend, had me cooking him slabs of bacon and six eggs every morning. He also smoked five packs of Camel Straights a day. Calculated at five minutes per cig, he would be a fat fire-breathing dragon nine solid hours a day. That's probably not a good idea for someone who weighed 350 pounds. Cigarettes and weight aside, he was the strongest man I had known up until that point.

When not out casting the net on unsuspecting salmon, I stayed in town, a village really. My father rented a house from Purple Paul, one-time Mayor of Craig, who needed all things to be purple, including the house, the interior walls, his clothing, hair, everything. It was like living inside of a black light poster.

I had made a few friends including a Native American girl I would pal around with. She had long, beautiful, raven black hair. On her next visit, she was wearing a stocking cap. Her brothers had cut her hair off with a hunting knife because of her association with me. She had been bleeding. I was horrified. My father thought it was hilarious. A real humanitarian, this was Ill Will at his best. It's the only one of two times in my life that I carried a gun. This one I appropriated from the pile of guns heaped under my father's bed. He had so many he never even missed it. I seriously contemplated shooting both him and the brothers.

Turtle Dick and Ill Will worked out a secret deal where the proceeds from my summer commercial fishing venture would go to my father. He had planned a mission to Saudi Arabia, possibly to teach alcohol education classes on the virtues of drinking to the Muslim population. I'm not quite sure. He had a lot of secret plans that only made sense to him. I found out about the secret deal through a third party who gladly ratted him out, and I was livid. I quit that job on the spot. I went on a hellacious bender, stole his no-water-pump-havin' panel wagon, ate some psilocybin mushrooms, loaded up my dog Tork, and headed for Seattle.

Chapter 18
The Right Side of the Tracks

The sign said, "No pets allowed. $250 a month." It was right next to the railroad tracks in the industrial Inter Bay neighborhood, a real shithole. It would be one of many.

"Perfect, I'll take it," I said.

As a testosterone laden twenty-something, I didn't even consider Tork a pet. My half Doberman, half German shepherd killer K-9 hybrid was a working dog there to protect my stash. He would bite holes through cans of dog food and squeeze the food out. I had strung up clothes lines all over the inside of the hovel and hung my pot plants upside down so the T.H.C. would run into the tips of the buds.

On day three of occupancy, I came home to a kicked-in door as Tork stood sentry, not a single bud was missing. Then later that week, the slumlord came around. Tork considered him an intruder. He latched firmly on to the landlord's man parts and gave him a guided tour of the property while I explained the pros and cons of sneaking up on me. Once again, the slumlord came around and forgot all about the no pet thing. He left me alone for the rest of my limited time there.

Like many a shithole, I wouldn't be there long. The treatment center circuit came a calling. I started the treatment center circuit at age twenty-one. Silver-haired Seattle Police Officer J.J. Fox had observed me geeked out of my fricken mind on coke between two buildings in the middle of the night.

"You might wanna look into that treatment thing," Officer Fox said while he burned his blazing flashlight into my expanding and contracting coke fiend pupils. He gave me a quarter and waited while I dialed the 24-hour number of a place called The Genesis House.

Behavioral modification was just the ticket, I guess. The very next day—because I had misbehaved—I was made to stand out in the street wearing a toilet seat around my neck with a sign that read "I'm an idiot." Welcome to rehab. Thankfully, they spared Tork the humiliation.

They'd make a gang of us stand out in front of a grocery store with a flier and beg for food. If you saw the shoppers' reactions as they read the flier you'd think it said "we're unpredictable and dangerous drug addicts, give us some food or we're going to have to rob you."

I'd have gone somewhere else, but they were the only ones who accepted pets. My dog Tork lived on one side of the yard, and Ear, the earless pitbull terrier, lived on the other side, both saw me through the treatment process. Fortunately, there's been a lot of progress in the addiction field since then.

The staffers did have some redeeming qualities. One time, they let four of us borrow the facility van so we could go bowling at the local non-alcoholic strip joint. I immediately fell in love with a stripper. After I proclaimed my love for the woman I wanted to spend the rest of my life with, and spending all our bowling money on dances, we dragged our dirty, sneaky, sorry asses back to the treatment center where the gig would soon be up. We were in serious trouble. Seems one of the female clients was an ex-stripper. We had all said way too much. The love of my life had ratted us out and took the treat right out of treatment.

We were all put in adult time-outs. We could only communicate by flash cards. I felt bad because Tork couldn't read. Once we redeemed ourselves, it was back to the business of group panhandling and humiliating sandwich boards.

Robert was my best friend in treatment and like a newly adopted big brother. He was a wealthy, low-bottom Aqua Velva man, which means he'd drink the aftershave for its alcoholic content. In 1981, Washington State liquor stores were closed on Sundays, so he had taxies deliver cases of Aqua Velva for his personal consumption and a very close shave. I'd never seen alcoholism to that degree. Later, I'd see plenty.

We lived directly across from a sorority house, so my mood began to improve. I had it in my head that I would meet my future highly educated, big-money wife, and she would take care of me while I drank and only smoked weed. Weren't all sorority girls looking for a guy just like me? "Get in line ladies." She would have needed the strength of a burro to schlepp all of the baggage I had accumulated.

Nate was lead wanker and a veteran of Genesis House. He was a handsome dipshit drug addict who knew how to turn on the charm. Robert, Ramy, Nate and I were upstairs adjacent to the sorority house making goo-goo eyes at the girls through their window across the alley. There were six or so young lovelies that giggled while they flashed us a little R-rated skin. This had been a regular occurrence with zero results, other than four pairs of cerulean blue-balls.

Nathan wasn't much when it came to being a man's man. He was only 130 pounds wet, with a fierce addiction to boot. But he had one talent. Nathan could fart on demand and took every opportunity to demonstrate this nifty magic trick. He was mighty pleased with himself. It was made possible by way of the endless supply of meaty, cheesy calzones his stout Italian mother provided him while visiting.

To impress the sorority girls next door, Nate took his trick to a new level. He turned his back to the window, dropped his drawers, lit a lighter and held it near his bared ass. As he blasted out a mega dose of hot Italian calzone juice, he set fire to his rectal flamethrower. It brought back memories of seventh-grade science class. He could have joined a circus.

"Holy fuck, that thing really works," Ramy said with glee as he jumped up and down at the sight and smells of scented flames pouring from Nate's backside.

Nathan screamed, "Aaaahhhhhhh," to the carcinogenic smell of his burning butt hairs.

Blowback.

This set off the fire alarm and the voice of God, in the form of Den Mother counselor Warden, boomed up the stairwell, "Who's smoking up there?"

Nate was definitely smoking up there. It made a decent little plume. Being an Italian he practically had an afro on his bum.

"Nice going Gasanova. Class act. There's gonna be a chick stampede up here any minute now," I said.

Robert finally accessed his voice and said, "What the hell Nate, we could have gotten laid."

"Ah, fuck them," Nate said, grimacing while trying to inspect the damage.

"That was the general idea," Robert said.

The girls were gone, most likely traumatized, and the room with a view remained empty from there on out. Nathan had deep fried his starfish, dashed our dreams and set fire to our desires.

I got a job at a deli mart/gas station midnight shift, fully disclosing my current situation and living arrangements to the owner. She knew she was taking a risk by letting a drug addict handle the till. Of course, I relapsed. I would lock the door, put up the BE BACK IN FIVE MINUTES sign and go do my hit. I would come back tweaking to an angry mob a half hour later. That was the pattern, a pattern that continued until the shift I worked on my birthday. I was tweaked out and for a happy birthday present, I got a gun stuck in my face. Judging from the barrel, it looked like a snub-nosed .38 to me. The thief probably stole it from a cop. He jumped the counter and helped himself to the till.

"Have a nice night," he said.

After the police came and reviewed the tapes, as well as my previous shift, the conclusion the owner came to was that I was somehow responsible. This is the one time I neither tapped the till nor was responsible though nobody else agreed with me.

Fired and down the road, I would flame out of Genesis House and the many treatment centers that followed, always trying to move as far away from myself as possible. I headed for greener pastures in sunny Southern California leaving scorched earth behind.

Piotter 92

Chapter 19
The US

Dave, a fellow escapee from the Genesis House Treatment Center, had won many blue ribbons for being a champion heroin addict. He was from southern California and familiar with the junkie landscape there. Talk about a guy hitting the skids! His parents were uber-wealthy real estate developers and lived in Dana Point, a well-to-do Southern California beach community. Dave had grown up in a house that sat high above the Pacific Coast Highway with a stellar view of the ocean. His folks were kind and generous people that he had managed to squeeze the life out of, as well as a multitude of greenbacks. So with a mission of adopting Dave's much talked about parents, I attached myself to the hull of his reeling ship and we sailed south in my 1969 AMC Rebel, the Walmart of car companies.

The Rebel was a sort of second-string muscle car and a close relative of the Pacer, which put the passengers on display under a glass dome. After a few minor scams, some good ole Yankee ingenuity, and panhandling, we cobbled together enough money for drugs, alcohol, gas, and corn dogs. Hells Angels' bathtub meth is a must-have for any junkie on vacation who passes through the Bay Area. After doing my first intravenous shot of meth, a new gorilla was born. I was accepted into the I.V. league. I nursed a half-gallon of straight Tanqueray gin and was in the land of milk, honey and heroin in no time.

As a young man and homeless—I'm talking about me—Huntington Beach wasn't a bad way to go: warm weather, plenty of unattainable eye candy, lots of Hacky Sack, more drug sack, plus free showers on the beach. It provided me with a whole new set of bridges to burn down.

As if to celebrate our arrival, mega rich kid and co-founder of Apple Computer, Steve Wozniak hosted a four-day music and cultural event in the San Gabriel Mountains called "The US Festival"—pronounced "us," as in "you and me." Four days of checking my brain at the door? I'm in. Off we went to my own personal Woodstock.

With aforementioned ingenuity, I scratched up enough dough to go, partially by my savings at the half-off store, where I came away with some shorts, a tank top, and a nice pair of flip flops. This was my idea of going-camping-up-in-the-mountains attire. (As it so happens, it does get cold in the California hills, just ask the Donner Party).

Ever the entrepreneurs, Dave and I gave away free hits of cheap acid with the purchase of some very expensive homemade, fake hash that consisted of sage and egg yolk for a binder. Once the acid kicked in, the fake hash was a nonissue for our clients. It allowed us to get paid for our product and not get killed in the process.

Van Halen was the headliner. The only act bigger at the festival was the band members' egos. After the crowd had slogged through Country Music Day and seen some stellar bands such as the Pretenders and Stevie Nicks, there was lead Hellion, David Lee Roth, wheeling his IV bottle of Jack Daniels around on the stage, insulting the crowd and pretending that he could sing. Even after a multi-day binge, I could tell he was failing miserably.

On the last day of the festival when the acid finally wore off, I discovered it was absolutely freezing! I had not noticed before, but in order to survive the night, I had to curl up next to a dumpster that was radiating heat from some road flares the state troopers had lit for some inexplicable reason. It was like they were shoveling coal to keep a train moving, there were thousands of them.

The sun rose, and I was on my own. Dave had spun off into the crowd a day earlier never to be seen again, by me anyway. My dream home and adopted parents spun off as well. The walk to the festival grounds from my car had been no less than five miles. I don't know why I had expected it to be any less going the other way. Nothing but a sea of cars. I was lost. The US Festival became the Poor Pitiful Me Festival.

Hours later, after almost all the other cars were gone, I finally spotted a red dot on the horizon. My atrophied muscle car never looked as tough as when I made my way toward it to drive back to my depressing reality. By the time I coasted down out of the San Gabriel Mountains back to the beach, both the car and I were out of juice.

I hadn't fully paid for that car before leaving the State of Washington. Because it was red and had out-of-state plates, it was an invitation to be pulled over by the California Highway Patrol. I waited until the plates expired and then I stripped the Rebel down and sold one part at a time. I left the rest up on blocks to be ravaged by the neighborhood's bone yard vultures. I lost sight of it forever on my hasty bus ride out of the state while once again trying to escape myself.

A true rebel without a cause.

Chapter 20
Hitched

Without my Rebel, my thumb became my go-to source of transportation. Fortunately, I had plenty of experience. For parts of two summers, my buddy and I hitchhiked east of the mountains to apple country near Lake Chelan to pick fruit and party. We would stand at the highway entrance with a cardboard sign that said "Lake Chelan" on one side and "Fuck You" spelled backward on the other. People would stop when they saw this, not always because they thought we were endearing. Even though we had to dive into the brambles a time or two, we would eventually get a ride.

Picking fruit is hard work. You have to go fast to make any money. I went fast, but I damaged a lot of fruit, thus joining the ranks of the unemployed. It seemed like I had already spent a lifetime picking in the hot sun prior to getting canned. In reality, it was probably one week.

I often prided myself on the fact that I never got a Driving Under the Influence citation. That's because they're not given for Walking Under the Influence. The car was always the first thing to be sold at the start of a coke binge, hence, the hitchhiking.

"Where are you going?" one fellow, who picked me up asked.

"I'm going to work. I own an auto mechanics shop, but my car is broke down."

It made perfect sense to me at the time. That's how out there I was.

Homeless and jobless at twenty-three was a particularly dark time in my life, dark enough that I took a Greyhound to Michigan. The bus, not the dog. My father was out there. Ill Will said the place teemed with high paying jobs. Landing one would be like shooting fish in a barrel, he bragged. I could write my ticket, he insisted. I had heard it before, but I was broke and dejected, so I drank his Kool-Aid one more time. This was pre-Lee Iacocca. The auto industry was in the shitter with the unemployment rate teetering at about fourteen percent. He must have been talking about the other Michigan.

Ill Will's latest scheme centered on what he did best: being loud. Upon my arrival, I found him demonstrating giant hybrid bullhorns to the local high school bandleader. Only my father could see the potential hidden value in these giant bullhorns. He had bought dozens of them at auction, another of his many "too good to pass up" deals. He hoped that this one sale would spark a buying frenzy where he would sell thousands of bullhorns to the townsfolk. The math suggested flaws in his plan, being that it was a town of five thousand. Everyone would have had to buy a six-pack. I tried to imagine a town that shouted their gossip about the neighbors at each other through these apparatuses as though this was to become the preferred mode of communication that would someday compete with cell phones. Grandma would no longer need that hearing aid.

Everything my father did involved loud.

With just one "maybe," buyer, I realized his goal for sales of these beauties were slightly on the lofty side. Like most things that involved Ill Will, I soon wanted no part of it. My one-week career as an assistant bullhorn huckster with my carnival-barker father ended my stay in Michigan. I stuck out my thumb and hitched back to Seattle.

On my way back west, deep in the vastness of Montana Big Sky country, I witnessed a crazy sight. Two adolescent males had escaped from a juvenile detention center, a military-style boot camp designed to tear one down and build them back up again. They were Hell bent on riding the rails out west to a big city, where it would take longer for their dreams to be crushed. After smoking cigarettes and listening to their plans, I watched from the road with my thumb out as they threw their meager belongings up onto the speeding locomotive. They tried to grab hold of the train at 50 miles an hour. It was harder than it looked. The result was two bruised prides and one broken hand. All they could do was wave goodbye and head back to boot camp as their polka dot handkerchiefs full of junk on a stick went on to a better life without them.

Chapter 21
Witness Protection Program

My first marriage was a disaster because I was a disaster. I traded my mom's couch for my soon-to-be wife's bed within a week of meeting her. I had appropriated my mom's couch after my week long nightmare in Michigan with my father. I would not recommend this style of courtship today if anyone were to ask. I convinced my wife-to-be that her life was about to change drastically. It did beyond what she could ever have imagined. She had been involved in a heavy-duty, black belt religion, think Bob Marley's God without the weed. How depressing. I learned that I'm not cut out to be a Jehovah's Witness. They seemed as relentless as pit bull terriers with no teeth.

When I found her, she was on the rebound from a marriage and had taken a break from the church tedium. I was just the guy to help her achieve sub-zero and shift the break from the church into a full-blown excommunication. On what was supposed to be her door-knocking day, I greeted a gaggle of her church cronies who came to pick her up at the door, which I answered in my bathrobe smoking a cigarette. I stated our need to celebrate Thanksgiving, which as it turns out, JWs don't do.

"So beat it," I told them.

Her fate was sealed, and she was temporarily excommunicated. I was thrilled with her progress.

Feeling good about nudging her in the right direction, I immediately set up a weed growing operation in her apartment. Lacquered pine troughs with automatic water pumps. Timers and lights with black plastic on all the windows. Fans and an exhaust system to blow the pungent smell out for the other tenants to enjoy. Power hooked up right from the source, bypassing the city's silly billing system.

After a series of highly predictable, yet catastrophic drug meltdowns, I scrapped the grow operation. We drove to Reno to get married. I then joined her church. The sequence of events were a little askew according to the church, but a whirlwind of activity none-the-less and the totally logical thing to do. They were happy to have us both back from Satan's clutches. God help me.

I attempted to make a show of it, half-heartedly going door-to-door with the other Pit Bulls as we offered up slices of salvation on Saturdays. I had gone door-to-door before for a carpet cleaning company. This felt quite similar and familiar, but not in a good way.

"Yes that's right Ma'am, your whole house cleaned as well as your dirty soul," I preached.

In reality it was more like, "Look, just read the stupid flier it's all in there!"

I had no takers.

I had trouble remembering and effectively delivering my lines. My poor hopeful converts looked at me like I was some kind of a drug addict or something.

I was neck deep in my religion as well as my disease and not thinking too clearly when Ill Will showed up on our tiny house's doorstep so he could celebrate our marriage and be the father he knew he could be.

I didn't quite know how he would react to the fact that my wife was black. Oddly enough, it was my mother who had a problem with it.

I remember her look of disappointment while saying, "What will my family think?" I knew she hadn't seen them in decades, so I didn't think they would think anything. I experienced prejudice from both sides and found it hard to navigate without total agitation. I wasn't mature enough to handle it; it greatly affected me.

My dad, after being dropped off at my house unannounced by a taxi, was thrilled, I guess.

"So you're the gal who saved my son," he yelled as he picked her up, spun her around and gave her a bear hug.

Ill Will intended to stay with us. I briefly considered the absurd and unattainable notion that I could reconnect with my father. Almost as soon as he arrived he asked, "Can I borrow your car for the day to run some errands?"

I had a moment of weakness and caved miserably.

The car was very small, and he was very large. His day of errands soon turned into a week. After his return from Reno where he married and divorced a casino, there was no trunk full of money. He did bring back a solar system of black holes in our cars upholstery, an ashtray bursting with butts and a permanently reclining bucket seat.

In addition to no apology or remorse, he no longer had a place to stay. My new bride's brief positive vibe toward Ill Will had vanished.

I continued to lead a double life. I developed a routine. I would drive around in my truck, duck below the dashboard and smoke cigarettes, paranoid that someone from the church would see me and rat me out. It got a lot worse fast. Everyone I saw was a potential Witness. I smelled rats everywhere.

My master plan of wife-as-savior unraveled fast. My double life became harder and harder to navigate. Try as she might, the challenge of saving me from myself was above my wife's pay grade. Though her efforts were Herculean, the notion that she could be equally insane did cross my mind. There's a program for that, too, as it turns out.

The jailhouse juggernaut was about to launch. My career as a JW fully fizzled after I robbed a 7-11 store with a socket wrench.

"Give me all the money or I will tighten your nuts."

I turned myself in. I surrendered to my higher power, the Seattle Police, and my short-lived salvation came in the form of an extended stay at the county jail. This would be my witness protection program though my troubles found me as fast as a Mob boss.

After I had settled into my new digs, my wife told me about a church elder who offered to divorce his wife to run away with her. I was still not adept at the art of self-control, so I vented my anger through threatening letters that I wrote from jail to said church elder. That finally tipped the scales for my soon-to-be-ex. I was deemed unsalvageable. Strangely, I developed a soft spot for that elder after I learned that, just like me, he ratted himself out and gave up his seat of power in favor of shame, humiliation, and his own divorce.

We were fortunate not to have owned anything except for my drug habit, which made for a quickie $90 divorce. She was a good-hearted person. I hope she found what she was looking for, if not in this life then after all Hell breaks loose in her next one.

Piotter 106

Chapter 22

Pumped

Don't mix pills and alcohol. I'd heard this sound advice a million times before but had never given it a serious thought because I was in the *rules don't apply* zone, plus I found the mix necessary if I were to endure. I got into the habit of taking whatever I could, as many as I could with alcohol, if I believed it would bring me down from all the cocaine, so I could sleep. My thought was that the stimulants would protect me from an overdose of the opiates and kind of level me out to normal as if I had taken nothing at all.

On the night I learned just why people are warned against the toxic mix, I didn't even know what pills I had taken, some kind of opiate I suppose. I never got a ride in a cop car that I didn't need or deserve, and this time was no different. They picked me up for public drunkenness on Highway 99. The cops asked me what was up. I answered honestly. I wasn't lucid enough to know I had anything to hide.

"Nothing much officer. I just took a bunch of pills and washed them down with some booze," I said.

My destination was not jail but Harborview Hospital, the Seattle hospital where all the addicts and indigents go to have their stomachs pumped, the pump house.

Cross this one off the bucket list. If you've never had this wonderful experience, the effect on the body is similar to the feeling of strychnine from blotter acid which turns your stomach inside out, but this has the added sensation of drinking a thumbtack smoothie. I realized I was lucky to be alive. My solution for the future was to shoot my dope in the emergency room parking lot just in case. My junkie mind started to fire on all cylinders.

The cost would only ratchet up in the weeks and months to come.

I don't know what the world record for heartbeats per minute is but my heart was pumping at 237. I felt like a winner. I was in a sleazy motel with my shooting gallery buddies when my heart spiked. I was on the verge of doing the fish in that motel room. Like addicts do best, they bugged out and left me for dead, but not before calling an ambulance.

"You guys are just aces," I said.

Bless their fast beating bleeding heartless hearts.

At that time in my life I spent an awful lot of time on Aurora Avenue North or at Harborview Medical Center, not what you would call upward mobility. First stop, emergency room. Second stop, fifth-floor psych ward for a five-day evaluation.

"Do you intend to harm yourself?" a very serious looking lab coat asked me.

"Yes, no, maybe," I rambled. "I don't know, let me the fuck out of here."

After five days of mild sedatives, whining sessions, wallet making, drooling and scoping out any possible women inmates who could make my life complete, I was kicked out and told to get my shit together and don't come back. How do you like that for gratitude?

Unlike ice, I didn't have my meltdowns when the sun was shining. No, mine always seemed to happen when it was cold outside. The clothing donation box outside Blessed Sacrament Church had the look of a reasonable spot for me to get warm, regroup and come up with a new and improved life plan. The only problem was there was already somebody else living inside. Harry the Hobo claimed ownership and gave me an eviction notice the moment I climbed in, but not before I set a spell to let my dust settle. He shared a can of Spaghettios with me that he got from the church food bank, damn they tasted good. Harry cooked them on a can of Sterno and then strained what was left of the Sterno through a T-shirt for an afternoon martini of sorts, leaving me shaken, but not stirred. He was an alcoholic's alcoholic.

"Waste not want not" was his motto.

When we finally decided to get out of our bunker, it was because of a small fire we had started inside. I guess I didn't see the "*no smoking*" sign. A chorus of church volunteers wailed in harmony at our arrival. The horror on their faces was memorable. Not one, but two smoking Lucifers burst out of that clothing bin. The fact that I was wearing the world's ugliest Christmas sweater that I had appropriated while inside the bin didn't help. I would get plenty used to people looking at me like that.

After the clothing bin debacle, we went our separate ways, and I endured a particularly difficult week of trying to stay loaded alone. Staying loaded was the most difficult job I've ever had. I was having a meltdown. Just as water seeks its level, it was not long before I found myself in the company of two other degenerate crack addicts I called Larry and Moe.

Urban camping had become the norm for me. I had surfed through all the couches I could. I was homeless. I traveled light so I wouldn't have to haul around a bunch of junk. The burden of ownership had become too much to bear. The daily grind was for suckers. I convinced myself that The Man wasn't going dictate my flight path. This was the pathetic lie I told myself as I whistled the guitar solo to Lynyrd Skynyrd's "Free Bird."

Larry wasn't really homeless. He could stay on the fishing boat that he worked on during the off-season. Moe, too, had options. He could stay at his parent's house, a perfectly decent God-fearing home in Moses Lake on the eastern side of Washington. These were my temporary crack buddies, my fellow travelers on the steep descent. Despite their housing options, they chose homelessness with me.

It was December, and it was twenty degrees outside. Shelter of any kind seemed like an attractive plan. The local homeless shelters were all full. They also required being born again between the hours of 6 p.m. and 8 p.m., which temporarily postponed the hunt for narcotics. That definitely wasn't going to work.

Larry claimed to have a friend who wouldn't mind if we borrowed his small trailer for some temporary shelter. So we tiptoed into Larry's friend's yard, and after respectfully not asking permission, we set off like yoked oxen and towed the Airstream Teardrop down Seattle's Burke Gilman Trail.

The Burke-Gilman Trail is a 27-mile long abandoned railway corridor that hugs the edge of Lake Washington. Free of vehicles, the trail is used by granola-eating individuals such as walkers, runners, and cyclists. We had a hard time blending in as we trudged the road with our Airstream. Having no set destination, we traveled two miles along the trail before setting up camp just off the trail and across from the Latitude 47, a five-star restaurant where we'd have access to a real bathroom and a water spigot. Just like Tom Joad.

I'd duck into the restaurant facilities, freshen up and do a couple of hand washables in the bathroom sink. After I discovered that drying boxers on a laundry line in December wasn't the most workable idea, I opted for the restroom's hand dryer and returned with clean, unfrozen clothes to the comfort of the propane heated Airstream. We were not so sure that the restaurant was thrilled with the good fortune of having us for neighbors. To their credit, the staff never called the cops.

The Teardrop was 8-feet long and 4-feet wide. This posed a challenge for bunking the three of us. We opted for sleeping head-toe-head. I did not want to be in the middle. Nevertheless, anyway we sliced it, we were each going to smell some feet.

The trail's bike and foot traffic was heavy; Seattleites like their exercise, turning our temporary digs into a hub of paranoia when we did drugs. My crack-induced hot flashes resulted in me shedding some of my clothes, shoes, socks and shirt at least. I always felt like I was suffocating after a hit of coke. The bundled up exercisers would see me half naked, tweaked out, and sweating in front of the Airstream despite the cold December air, a site that surely jogged their minds while they jogged their bodies.

We soon concluded that the unsavory outdoorsy element was a detractor to our junkie lifestyle and decided it was time to move on. We packed up our carnival, returning the caravan semi-safely to its rightful owner and set off to borrow a Lincoln.

Chapter 23
The Three Wise Men

Larry, Moe and I formulated a plan—after breaking into a car wash change machine and scooping out about one hundred dollars' worth of quarters with a soup ladle—to drive to Moses Lake, two and half hours east of Seattle. We were convinced we would soon become the toast of the town.

Toast *in that* town was more like the way it worked out.

It was the night before Christmas Eve (no, this ain't no fairy tale) and we needed wheels to get to Moses Lake. I latched on to the idea that Larry's grandma was old and that she wouldn't even notice her missing sled. That calmed my conscience. It was the only Christmas gift we were gonna get. So we stole her old Lincoln Continental. We gassed up, found a drug dealer who accepted quarters in the middle of the night and set out over Interstate 90 in the attention grabbing, "oh so slow" lane and headed to Moses Lake.

We arrived in Moses Lake at daybreak to find ten inches of snow on the ground. We parked the Lincoln in front of an abandoned house. Larry decided to relieve himself, like any dog would do, on a telephone pole under the disapproving eye of the Neighborhood Watch Captain.

After a hot meal and a heartfelt homecoming on Christmas Eve at Moe's parents' house, the three of us, all over the age of thirty, got tucked into our sleeping bags on their floor. While drifting off to sleep, we wondered what Christmas surprises would be waiting for us next morning under the tree until we were jolted awake by what was a familiar sound to me.

"Sheriff's department. Open up!"

As for what I was going to get for Christmas? My question was immediately answered. I got a felony! What did you get?

We hadn't exactly been geniuses at covering our tracks. Barney Fife could have solved this one. It seems the police ran the Lincoln plates and then followed our footsteps in the snow right to our door. Grandma was a little sharper than I had given her credit for. The litany of "if onlys" was endless that Christmas morning: If only Larry could have held his bladder, if only I wasn't a crack addict, if only she really was Larry's grandma, if only I didn't steal that car, if only. The official charge was "taking a motor vehicle without the permission of the owner," which sounded a lot less guilty than "grand theft auto." But it was a felony nonetheless and good for thirty days in county lockup. It was my second of five felonies and the beginning of my relationship with Grant County Jail.

During booking, Moe requested I take the wrap because he had important things to do.

"Wake up and do your time," I said, ever the veteran jailbird in my mind.

A fight ensued. We were both a couple of featherweights. We flailed our emaciated arms and inflicted no damage.

As it so happened, Moe's dad was the jail chaplain. He would play guitar and sing songs that offered me the promise of a crack-free tomorrow via salvation from the error of my ways through the blood of the lamb. I was looking for free crack tomorrow. I found it confusing, thinking maybe he was referring to the road-kill fed to the inmates. I may have taken him up on it if he'd have been offering beef, I considered lamb a little too gamey. The chaplain dad didn't seem to care too much for his own son Moe and offered him neither salvation, lamb, beef, nor bail. He had long since been tapped out.

Chapter 24
De-Construction Site

I had entered the junkie realm of a total paranoiac alternate universe. Gone were the days when it was a casual, fleeting thought that maybe someone was 'out there' and after me. If you've ever seen the Francis Ford Coppola movie *The Conversation* starring Gene Hackman, you have an idea of what I'm saying. I was bugged, and I was determined to get to the bottom of it. Paranoia is a prevalent trait amongst cokeheads deep into their disease like I was.

Brian had a habit of keistering his stash so he wouldn't have to share it with other free loading junkies. So close, but yet so far away. As bad as I was, if offered, I'd have had to decline. I still had a sliver of self-respect and had to draw the line somewhere. Brian related that he had stuffed himself inside a dryer for six hours to escape his imagined detection. It's not like I could look down my drug-fueled paranoid nose at him. I tried to crawl inside a cold air vent to escape my own.

Carpet crawling was another ugly trait that afflicted me. One hit of dope and I was instantly down on all fours with the rest of the bugs looking for that minute particle that could potentially bring me upright again.

Sick.

Never make the mistake of finding a diamond ring in a sleazy motel while smoking crack, like I did, just in case you were thinking about doing that. The after-effect put me in a constant state of looking for non-existent hidden treasures or equally non-existent listening devices. I would focus my eyeball on the key-hole of the door, stock still for thirty minutes or so until I was sure either my eyeball would explode or that the G-Men weren't going to blast through the door. Very carefully, like the game of Operation, I would dissect the switch plate covers, base molding and light fixtures. I'd pull up carpets and take apart the pea traps under the sinks looking for the microphone or possibly something of greater value. The search often resulted in a trashed and dismantled room.

These motel rooms were a few rungs down from a Motel Six, more like a Motel Ten. I'm not sure they could have been damaged. After burning through the last glimmer of dope and re-comporting myself, I would determine that it had been a false alarm. Always careful, I reversed the order and Voila! Ready for the next down-and-outer to repeat the whole ugly process. Little did I know I was practicing for my sober residential remodeling career, skills that have since served me well.

Tearing up motel rooms and coming down from a near fatal high builds an appetite. I went to my friend Denny's house to grab a bite.

"Whad'll ya have?" Flo asked.

Flo was the formidable, sturdy-framed Denny's waitress who, armed with pencil and pad sidled up to my table. She was in her zone. At that moment, I thought maybe I'd like to have a new life or possibly some cash to cover the obscene meal I was about to order.

The temple of Denny's Restaurant, often a true spiritual experience, if only for entertainment value, offers a full-service breakfast at all times of day. On this night, it was 2 a.m.

"I'll have steak and eggs, pancakes, toast, sausage, bacon, coffee, juice," I said.

Flo scribbled furiously and had to interrupt me to sharpen her pencil,

"Some pie, and hash browns. That pretty much covers it, and, oh, keep the coffee coming."

I could have expedited things by simply pointing at the menu and stating "one of each." Ordering like this sure beat posing as a busboy and asking, "Are you through with that?"

I would have ordered some booze too, to take the edge off, but that required money up front.

It had been about 72 hours since my last meal, and the only thing I had been chewing on during that time were my fingernails. To the astonished onlookers' surprise, I had not ordered for a party of five. I made light work of the digestive disaster before me.

About an hour and a half after my maximum mandible workout, I was nodding off in the comfort of my floral patterned vinyl Denny's bench seat, when, with a gentle nudge, Flo snapped me back into the reality of my dismal life.

"Will there be anything else?" she asked.

"Flo, I've got to be honest with you," I said. "I don't have two nickels to rub together. You might as well call the cops."

At the time, to me, there was barely a distinction between jail and treatment. Both were temporary respites from the ever-present shit-storm on my gloomy horizon. Flo's compassionate eyes and lack of surprise as she sized up my massive 135-lb. chemical makeup and all-black suicide wardrobe indicated she already suspected as much.

"O.K. Getcha some more coffee?" she asked.

Though chiseled from granite, Flo had a soft spot. God bless Flo. After bumming a smoke from her, I felt compelled to steal a tip for her off another table. Fascinated with my complementary Denny's toothpick, I settled in for my just deserts while the other patrons enjoyed the show.

The Seattle Police often get a bad rap, but my lengthy experience with them has been generally positive. After kickin' my ass, they always managed to protect my head while stuffing me into the patrol car.

The men in blue appeared at my table.

"What's going on?" they asked Flo.

"Hungry crack head," I replied coming out of my slumber in full anticipation of my punishment.

But this was a rare instance where I did not go to jail when the police were involved. These two channeled the spirit of Saint Flo, the patron saint of dine-and-dashers and instead took me to detox to come down off the drugs and my grand slam breakfast before I headed to the comfort and compassion of Cedar Hills Treatment Center.

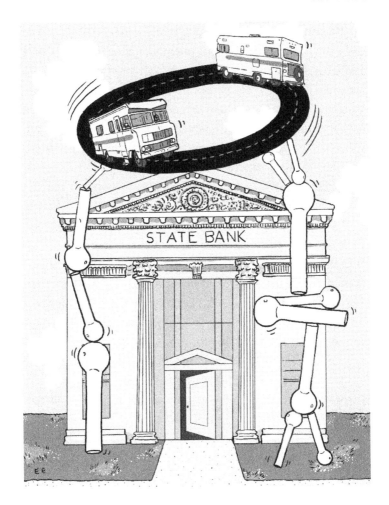

Chapter 25
Mini Winnie

When thinking to myself, "what's the perfect getaway vehicle?" I imagined something fast: maybe a Beemer, a Porsche, or even something less flashy like a Camry. I never really considered having to settle for the raw power and pinpoint maneuverability of a Winnebago. But there you have it. Desperate times call for desperate measures.

This beast was owned by Herb, a divorced, retired mechanic and the current husband of "Ruth," a workin' girl whose stage name now escapes me. Ruth had pimped Herb out. She steered him from social crack dabbler to full-blown addict. He had cashed in his white picket fence and followed her down the rabbit hole.

I had fallen down my own rabbit hole, a detour I had taken on the way home after the summer salmon season of 1990. In a rare moment of trying to pull myself together I returned to Alaska to fish and made some good money. I had big plans on returning home a conquering hero. On the way, I stopped for one drink, and it was one too many. The days blurred together; the Benjamin Franklins disappeared, and I became a member of Herb and Ruth's traveling road show. My last glimmer of normalcy was definitely in the rearview mirror. The next three years would become my thousand-day nightmare.

My newfound companions had an open marriage. The Winnebago was their happy home and traveling bordello. Among her tricks, she claimed the ability to suck a golf ball through a garden hose before losing a lung to crack. Though a formidable feat, I could not see the value in it, being a service that few requested.

In the wheelhouse, Captain Herb was stiff with fear while navigating the mean streets. The stress of signaling on every turn so as not to break the law took its toll, while in the back, Ruth, a journeyman hooker, serviced her johns. I was not one of them. I didn't want to be bothered with a distraction like sex for money while smoking crack, nor could I had I wanted to. I just wanted some company, folks equally pathetic as I upon whom I could unleash my tale of woe, people who would acknowledge what a scumbag I had become and affirm my lowly self-image. The happy newlyweds were eager to help. My association with them would prove to be an expensive counseling session.

We had logged forty-eight hours and five hundred miles within a five-mile radius when I realized I needed to take care of some business.

"Pull over, I've got to cash a check," I said.

"No problem," they said in stereo, boring holes in me with their crack-hungry eyes.

For two days, they had helped me burn through a sizeable bankroll, so they believed there really was a check to cash.

"I'll be back in a flash," I said.

It's a sinking feeling when you play tug of war with a bank teller, especially over the holdup note. I had written this particular note on a legitimate check stub that had my name on it. I had to give her and the surveillance camera the stink eye to get it back and avert disaster.

Upon my return to Hell on Wheels with a fist full of dollars, the honeymooners had a momentary freak-out at the realization that they were unsuspecting accomplices in a bank robbery and thus, *really* breaking the law. They went through the five stages of greed: greed, envy, rage, forgiveness, euphoria, and greed. I neutralized their discomfort with the promise of a drug bounty. And the crack angels sang.

Like dogs returning to their own vomit, we were off to Highway 99, Seattle's Aurora Avenue North. Urban decay had turned a once vibrant business community into a thoroughfare of dealers, junkies, prostitutes, cheap motels and worst of all, used-car salesmen. We got what we came for. With curtains drawn, stash replenished, and our hippocampi flooded with dopamine, we decided to hit the road to see America from the inside of a smoke-filled aluminum box.

The normal two-and-a-half hour trip to Yakima over the mountains into Eastern Washington took about ten hours, seven and a half of which was tweak time. We picked up a fellow traveler along the way. C.Z. was an old gangster who claimed to be the seventh son of a seventh son, a variety of life coach, prophet or some such shit. Everything about this guy was phony except for the fact that, like me, at this point in his life he was a *real* loser. Prior to joining our circus, he had been high on the mountaintop fasting on malt liquor and menthol cigarettes. His intention was to gain access to my crack.

Clarification: the drug, not my orifice.

We stayed up all night and burned the pipe at both ends.

Like putting quarters in a jukebox, this trio sang my praises as long as the crack nuggets flowed. After we had shoveled the remainder of the bank money into the glass pipe incinerator and moved on to wine-in-a box, I ditched the crack whisperers and their mobile snatch unit in Yakima.

Emptied of every thought in the aftermath of my binge, I was both clueless and rideless. I stuck out my thumb and hitchhiked west, back across the mountains. A Good Samaritan, who picked me up, asked if I had broken down.

I nodded and proclaimed "On a massive scale."

He too was a little clueless and figured I was a trucker in need of a mechanic. Then his light bulb came on, which put the brakes on any further conversation. I welcomed the silence.

Good Sam deposited me back in the Emerald City where I called my lifelong buddy J.P. Much to my consternation, J.P. had gotten sober a year earlier. Through blistered lips and an addled brain, I told him what I had done at the bank.

"You can't tell anyone, we can get through this," he said.

I agreed, then immediately turned myself into the Seattle Police Department.

This wasn't the first time I had turned myself in for a crime I had committed. I was practically an honorary detective. I hoped being a crime fighter and criminal all rolled into one would appeal to the judge and have a positive effect on my sentencing. Such hope was short lived. So I opted *not* to address the court on sentencing day with "Afternoon, Your Honor, I've solved another crime." I exercised my right to remain silent.

"Mr. Piotter, you can't keep committing crimes and turning yourself in expecting leniency from the court," the judge said.

Thus began what would be a long slog and intimate relationship with the penal system.

I felt I had dodged a bullet by turning myself in. I was charged with second-degree robbery, my first prison sentence: state time, nineteen months. This would be considerably less time than the feds were handing out for the same thing, as I would learn in a few short years. Brilliant.

Some people join the military; I joined prison. I thought a little discipline and exercise in my life might do me some good.

I didn't occur to me that I could have just joined a gym.

.

Chapter 26
Go West Young Man

I had lived in Seattle most of my life before I ever set foot into West Seattle. Seattle was named after Chief Sealth of the Duwamish tribe. The purpose for my sudden urge to explore wasn't in the interest of local history or geography; it was drugs and crime, pure and simple. My new favorite neighborhood was a predominately family-oriented Hispanic community with ties to the Mexican mafia who prided themselves on cocaine quality.

After finishing my state sentence, I got out and went back to the streets. I arrived on the West Seattle scene with the scariest ex-con I had known up 'til then. T-Bone Mosey had a habit of carrying a loaded .45 with him and threatening whoever it was he was doing drugs with while rushing from a mainline jolt of cocaine. I was on the receiving end and was amazed to still find my head attached to my shoulders after being dragged around in a headlock at gunpoint. I became the focus of his paranoia. Us against them had somehow become him against me. I literally dodged a bullet.

Prior to that, the last time I saw T-Bone was in the state work release. I had a free pass to abuse heroin via a doctor-prescribed opiate for an on-the-job injury. I chose to share my good fortune with T-Bone. We were shooting dope in his room at the state work release when the goon squad came crashin' through the door. I stepped behind the door leaving T-Bone to be hauled off back to prison. I tiptoed out from behind the door when the coast was clear and temporarily ratcheted my behavior back a notch. When I saw him again a year and a half later, I became his sidekick. Everyone could use a good sidekick.

I had a $500-a-day habit and no income. I was totally unemployable. My only option was crime, which I did until the wheels came off my flaming wagon. In hindsight, it's unbelievable to me what I went through to keep loaded. I've worked on the docks, road construction, commercial fisheries, carpenter, lumber mill and more, and by far, hustling dope one hit at a time is the hardest job I've ever had.

As a cokehead, heroin addiction looked pretty good to me. I had never seriously done it. My skewed logic was that heroin addicts can relax, eat a meal and they don't have to stab themselves with a needle every ten minutes or crawl around on the floor. It sounded better than what I had been used to. I added it to my repertoire of toxins and started doing speedballs, a combo of cocaine and heroin intravenously, also known as Belushis. This power cocktail of drugs made famous by the deceased comic genius provided the impetus for my trek to West Seattle. Soon, I too was a cracked out smacked out resident of West Seattle's felony flats.

It was like old home week my first week there. I reconnected with long-lost fiends. Pauline was a heroin addict, a dealer I had met in state work release. While on the freeway, Pauline had been hit in the face by a flying chunk of metal that came off of the back end of a truck. The metal broke her jaw and helped launch her into her own personal opium wars, which she fought for years. We met in the state coed halfway house where we became as thick as thieves. She became one of a growing list in my crime co-op and was conveniently located right across the streets from a human tick named Toxic Stu.

My crimes didn't always go as planned. Once, after pinching a 7-11 for two cartons of Newports, my accomplice slash driver assured me of the 50 cents on the dollar we would get in High Point, a low-income housing project in West Seattle that I had no business being in. He failed to tell me that he was at the high point of High Point's most wanted list for ripping off a gangbanger. Those dudes had guns, but unlike Elvis Costello, their aim was not true. After they unloaded what seemed like a Costco-sized gun clip, they allowed me to steal another day.

The box of oysters was not my finest hour. It was just a means to temporary relief. There were forty-eight, eight-ounce containers of raw oysters on ice in front of a mom and pop seafood store in a cardboard box. It was 6 a.m., and I got on the bus with that leaking box cradled in my lap, headed for Chinatown and its open-air black market. I unloaded all forty-eight for about a buck a piece, but not before getting warned from a King County health inspector who told me to "get the fuck lost." End result: twenty miles covered and one small hit of dope. All this only took about six hours. All in a day's work.

Times like these nudged me towards bank robbery. These days my work often takes me into the old stompin' grounds. The names and faces have changed, but the activities in the White Center area are the same. I'm certain of that.

Chapter 27

The Booster Club

There were benefits to being skin and bones. Food budget aside, I could stash copious quantities of merchandise on my body where fat and muscle used to be. Better boosting through starvation. I'm not talking about someone who supports athletic programs, I'm talking about stealing merchandise, though I would have welcomed the support of some fundraisers as my daily drug habit was becoming more and more difficult to sustain by myself. As my tolerance level and need for larger quantities of narcotics grew, so grew the amount of merchandise I boosted.

Go team!

My existence was like bad math. The more drugs I needed, the more crime I did. They escalated while my life continued its fall in the opposite direction. I became the "go-to-guy" when setting off in a jalopy full o' junkies. I never returned empty handed. K-Mart was easy pickins, as they had a no-receipt return policy. Junkies practically bumped into each other inside those stores. If you hit all seven in the Puget Sound area you could coast through the night. Silk shirts were always a favorite because you could boost twenty at a time. They didn't take up much space, and Mexican drug dealers loved them.

"May I take your order please," I'd ask.

They'd send me out with a long list to fill. Fill it I would.

Hummels, those cutsie little German porcelain figurines, were worth a little money and easy to conceal too. They were a temporary answer to my junkie prayers. The Merry Wanderer, School Boy and Puppy's Bath: At thirty cents on the dollar these bad boys could keep me off the streets for a couple of days.

My new fence lived in White Center on the main drag, 16th Ave. S.W. in the shopping district right next to the King County Sherriff's Office, just in case anyone tried to steal his stolen stuff. A used appliance store was his front, but I believe he came by being a fence honestly. I would schlepp my stolen merchandise into his office and he would feel so sorry for me being a pathetic junkie that he would make an exception and take whatever it was off my hands and allow me to temporarily "get well." Multiply that by scores of similar sad sack thieves and Voila! A bleeding hearted fence. He did have to be careful because on the other side of the wall the cops were face down in their donuts. He didn't want to wake them from their sugarcoated slumbers.

I once walked in carrying a Remington double-barreled hunting rifle with a Leopold oscillating scope that I had appropriated from Joe, who was making the transition from respectable to susceptible. It was totally concealed inside a sleek carrying case.

Despite its sleekness, the case was the exact shape of a rifle. Still, I felt invisible. The locals didn't bat an eye, but the fence was less thrilled. Not wanting any guns on the premises, he sent me packing. I headed out and down the road with my not-so-invisible rifle on the hunt for narcotics. Now that's going to any lengths.

I often poured over the neighborhood newspaper want ads to see if there was anything I could tap into that would put some dope in my spoon. This ad read, "Looking for a Remington double barrel rifle and Leopold oscillating scope. Top dollar."

By golly, I happened to have had one of those and had been toting it around for days. My stopgap prayer had finally been answered. With the promise of a payout from the sale of this much talked about legendary rifle, I had collected about four dope-less junkie barnacles to come along for the ride.

"I'll be back shortly," was never an acceptable response to the odd man out.

We piled five deep into a 1970 Toyota Corolla with the rifle in tow. Toxic Stu insisted we make it six and said he was willing to ride in the miniature trunk. We outvoted him five to one. He hung on to the door handle, whined and begged for as long as his smoldering size eleven Chuck Taylors burned off the last of their tread. I experienced great pleasure while we dragged him down the street.

Chapter 28
Den of Vipers

The Joe Michael Apartments were a tidy low-budget West Seattle affair that housed California Avenue's working poor and the occasional no-account junkie scumbag thrown in the mix. It was also home to widely vilified Toxic Stu. I hated Toxic Stu. Being around Toxic Stu became a necessary evil, like emptying your bowels. Stu was a real asshole. All the bidets in Europe wouldn't make that guy clean. But unlike most of the other junkies I knew, he did happen to live indoors. Compared to the company he kept, he lived quite comfortably.

He was a barely upright, barely alive or breathing R. Crumb cartoon character, lanky with the posture of a question mark and a Dutch boy haircut. As a master scumbag, he was always quick to flaunt the fact that he was a fully funded heroin addict. He was spoon fed in more ways than one. His benefactor father and grandmother allowed him to avoid the miserable daily hustle that us lowbrow addicts endured.

I seriously hated that fucking guy. Stu's Dad was an executive at Alaska Airlines who had humiliated himself by wrestling with the drunken and verbally abusive Toxic Stu at a company party. His punishment for spicing things up at Dad's expense was exile to heroin-riddled West Seattle and the Joe Michael Apartments where he would fly the fiendish skies. The checks kept rolling in so long as Stu stayed far away. My bet was that Dad hoped for an accidental overdose death so he could consider Stu paid in full, but everyone who knew him knew he had the constitution of Keith Richards. Grandma, who was on her way out and barely with it, still viewed Junior as a lovable eight-year-old. She was conveniently located right up the street and took care of the food and cigarette money.

As Lord of the Fleas, life had its advantages as far as Toxic Stu was concerned. He would lay about drinking and smoking cigarettes, berate whoever happened to have just left his den while waiting for the next hit of dope to walk across his threshold. His junkie world-view was summed up as, "What's yours is mine and what's mine is mine."

I once smashed him square in the face with a metal garbage can lid. I instantly felt regret, not because I injured him, but because I hadn't. Thanks to his usual saturation of pain meds, he barely noticed.

His apartment was on the A-list of West Seattle "shooting" galleries and it was always packed. The cover charge added to his lavish junkie lifestyle. Most shooting galleries were without running water. This posed a problem when you needed to liquefy your dope for intravenous use. Stu's was a boutique gallery, and oddly enough, quite tidy with plenty of running water. He was a dirty clean freak. Upon entering, everyone would be given a spic-n-span cleaning task. Most had never even seen a cleaning product. After a quick tutorial, they scoured everything in sight so they could get on with the business of using their dirty syringes. With the Commander-in-Thief breathing down their necks, it was a slow moving beehive of opiated cleaning activity. I'd only been involved in slowly killing myself up to this point. But Stu motivated me to seriously consider the merits of homicide. Ultimately, I realized that helping Stu check out would not serve my higher self.

This revelation was a major disappointment.

Not once did I run into the likes of Miles Davis or Jack Kerouac advocating the merits of heroin addiction in any of the shooting galleries I frequented. The days of being a genius and being on heroin would never apply to me. Absolutely nothing artistic goes on at all aside from counting the multi-layered burnt skin sculpture between Stu's fingers that grew worse every time he nodded off on heroin while smoking. Though my route was misguided, a quest for normalcy through chemicals was really what I was on. I always considered myself a stand-up, caring and compassionate junkie thief.

Twelve years later as a construction contractor I was sent on a service call to that very apartment. I wouldn't have been surprised if Stu had answered the door with a bottle of bleach and an empty spoon like a junkie cockroach that had survived a nuclear holocaust.

Chapter 29
Double Your Misery

There had been much discussion of "The Twins" at the Viper's den shooting gallery, one of the countless drug dungeons where I had been wiling away the hours before my imminent demise. The Twins were known by reputation as identical-twin African American male drug dealers. Brother brothers. I had doubted their existence and rated them right up there with the junkie unicorn before witnessing these mythical creatures for myself.

The Twins took the 2 to 6 a.m. shift catering to the desperate dope fiends that popped up like mushrooms after dark. This was their niche. As drug dealers went, they were considered bottom feeders, but they took all forms of currency, even Canadian nickels. Though it was the summer of 1993, these two seemed to be about a generation behind the times with their Shaft-style wardrobe choices: Wide-lapelled, Naugahyde trench coats trimmed with fake fur and gleaming Afro Sheen-treated coifs topped off with plaid fedoras. They may have been on a twenty-year binge unaware of what decade they lived in. At the time, I considered their nifty getups a step up from the hand-me-downs I wore.

Their shit was far from "The Shit." It had barely enough legs to walk you over the bridge to daylight when you could get your hustle on and cop some real dope, but for a junkie in the wee hours, it would have to do.

The Twins sold heroin and cocaine cut with Enfamil powdered baby formula, which, in combination with the drug itself, would have an immediate synergistic "shit your pants" effect. Not that anyone cared or even noticed in the dark and dingy world I lived. I was a go-fast kind of junkie, but I desperately needed to wind down. I hoped for some black tar heroin to screw up my courage and rob another bank at 9 a.m.

Black tar was notoriously dirty and often good for a potential limb-losing abscess if the user didn't properly filter or missed a vein. Being armed with this knowledge was never enough of a deterrent for me. Like Domino's, The Twins delivered in thirty minutes, but unlike Domino's, it was never free. Any seasoned Seattle junkie knew you shouldn't buy white powder from a black dude in White Center.

You could tell if a drug dealer was their own best customer by the quality of the product, their hours of operation, the condition of vehicle and general appearance, not to mention the existence or absence of soap and water. I never saw The Twins' car and don't know if they even owned one. They could have been traveling on badass pogo sticks as far as I knew. I do know that those guys, like me, were on the one hit at a time getting loaded program.

Stolen merchandise was always tradable with The Twins. They would take anything as long as it was new. They had some swap meet thing going on in daylight hours. I was usually half drunk when dealing with the twins. Seeing double in their presence sure wouldn't help my end of the negotiations any. Now there were four of them. Their dope sacks were always light, but according to The Twins, less was always more. They must have been on the metric system. The math always favored the Twins. With a tradable value of twenty cents on every retail dollar for the stolen goods and their dope being only about twenty percent in purity, they got a lot of cash and a junkie got what amounted to shit. Even less after den mother Toxic Stu got his cut. It was just enough to make me cry and then jones for more.

Seeking goods to pay the Twins, I learned the Pay 'n Pak hardware store's cargo container sat full at the dock—a fact I'd discovered while out being a night crawler. I weighed about 130 pounds and that meant, like Houdini, I could weasel my way up and into the narrow space between the container and the building. My head must have been shrinking. After I lowered myself down and out with the

merchandise, I walked back down the alley to the Vipers'
den. I was amazed at how fast I made the one-mile trek. I
was like a speed donkey on a mission. I had a bed sheet
bigger than me, stuffed full of about a hundred pairs of
leather driving gloves and six or seven giant, oscillating fans.
I chose the fans because they were the only items as trim as I
that could make their escape with me.

It was August and as it turned out the fans were a viable
street commodity, especially amongst the profusely sweating
coke fiend crowd who seemed to be everywhere in the
neighborhoods I frequented. All you needed was an
electrical outlet, though due to unpaid electric bills, not
always available and for many, an afterthought.

"How you make this thing work, dog?"

I heard this more than once on the streets.

"You got to spin the blades brother, spin the blades!"

Waiting what seemed an eternity behind a handful of
other desperate junkies to conduct my bad business, I finally
stepped up to the trough.

Like any identical twins worth their weight in baby
formula, these guys, whose real names were unknown,
possibly even to themselves, finished each other's sentences.

"We got grams, teeners, and 8-balls," one said.

"Black and white, anything," another said

"You need," the other finished.

"We take cash, credit, merchandise and booty."

"Whachoo got?"

Two pairs of identical eyes laser focused on my loaded
bed sheet.

"Fans and gloves," I said.

I took comfort in the fact that the only booty belonging
to me being discussion was wrapped up in the sheet.

"We'll take all that shit," they said after examining the merchandise.

My world had become inundated with shit. I traded mine for theirs. With my empty sheet acting as my security blanket, I hung on until daylight came so I could repeat the cycle to survive another day.

Chapter 30
Lift Off

As a homeless junkie, I knew I was going to be covering some serious ground and have to run very fast to service my addiction. A comfortable pair of sneakers was just the ticket. In my daily hustle, it wasn't difficult to cover thirty miles on foot in a day. The reason my photo was in the offices of the Bon Marche' wasn't because I was loved and admired by the staff but despised and vilified. They may have gotten tired of me parking my worn out dog sleds next to the Air Jordans. I was in and out, a pair for me and one for my Jones. I'm pretty sure my shoulder was separated after being body slammed in the middle of Fourth Avenue by these young hulk style crime fighters who worked security. Bless their souls they had a hard job keeping up with the likes of me.

Toxic Stu's apartment was full of stranded passengers waiting for a connecting druggie flight. I had stolen Michael T's car in the middle of the night in preparation for my 9 a.m. withdrawal, which left a houseful in limbo. For Michael T, a Benjamin Franklin meant all was forgiven and help was on the way.

My motto was "if it ain't broke, don't fix it." I hit the same bank that morning that I had robbed three years earlier in the Winnebago. This would soon be indictment number one of eleven. The next ten would get a whole lot easier as my balls grew in direct proportion with my drug habit.

We piled into Boatie's car for a mini tour of the island directly following my pathetic bank takedown, a vacation, from my vacation from reality. Boatie and Debbie were old heroin addicts from Vashon Island, maybe the only two that had ever lived there and in my mind they both deserved a likeness in bronze. Boatie had once been a Merchant Marine before his personal slide into the giant spoon. His current boat was a 1969 Plymouth Fury nine-passenger station wagon. It was as much of a wreck as he was. I had purchased a half-ounce of coke and two grams of black tar heroin for the ride. I would need every bit of it. There was Billy J., Squinny, Becky, Michael T., myself, Toxic Stu, Boatie, and Debbie. I felt like a Mother Robin passing out worms. It was a Saturday in August, with real people loading the ferry boat doing real things. Maybe we could've passed for a family from somewhere, but we never got out of the car, never even rolled down the windows. The thing that probably saved us from arrest was the thick fog of cigarette smoke, which prevented any passerby from catching a glimpse of our mad scene. There were a lot of bumping elbows with all the dope being shot and spilled en route to paradise imagined. We made the seventy-five-mile loop around the island managing to avoid anything of interest as our attention was focused solely on the task at hand. As Carly Simon had said, "Nobody does it better."

Chapter 31
Pay It Forward

The sub creatures I shared addictions with often circled the same drain. I met up with Ruth again— about two years after our crack induced Winnebago bank robbery escapade. My previous uninformed getaway driver Captain Herb was replaced by "new and improved" future ex-husband, Jack. Herb had broken down for good and was scrapped along with the R.V. Ruth and I had both reemerged back on the scene at about the same time. She returned from dismantling Herb and his Winnebago, plus a long stint in treatment. I returned from serving my first prison sentence. We all shared delusions of grandeur fueled by Jack Daniels' Tennessee whiskey. Jack, Ruth's new disposable husband, was the driving force behind our new business plan. Money man Jack, with his mighty resolve, was going to be stronger than Herb and build himself into the next Pablo Escobar, a drug kingpin feared by all. Jack knew he would be all-powerful once he built up his cocaine empire. One has to start somewhere, so he started with what looked to me like about an ounce of pure cocaine and a quart of Tennessee bourbon.

Since our last visit included me funding Ruth's honeymoon with a week-long coke binge, she enlisted me to help strip Jack clean of all his coke and dignity. Being a former stripper, she knew how to strip. That was her way of paying it forward.

In a drunken blackout, Jack enlisted the help of his "loyal" wife as the gatekeeper of the stash. In his mind, she would be the logical choice to help him reach the pinnacle because she knew the ins and outs of the business. Ruth, in turn, enlisted my help for different reasons. She had trouble finding a vein on her own. No longer turning tricks, she needed something to occupy her time if only for a few hours.

The gist of what I said to Jack was, "Jack, I would be honored to be assistant director of marketing for your product line. Why, under the direct tutelage of Ruth, it's a slam-dunk. How could we go wrong?" Let me explain.

This somehow made sense in Jack's Jack Daniels state of mind.

All smiles, Ruth and I were both thinking "have a nice nap now, and we'll see you in about fourteen hours after our intensive strategy session bears fruit."

We had much to do, talking, planning, dreaming, drumming up customers, counting money, buying cars, taking vacations and eventually chopping and weighing and divvying and packaging and testing and shooting and smoking. Divide and conquer.

"My look at the time, what day is it," I said as the sleeping giant stirred.

We were both voracious abusers. We helped Jack get down to his right size lickity split. There were way too many problems to be solved by one measly bag of dope, and all three of us relied heavily on it. By the time he came to, there was barely enough stash left to beat the junkie freeloaders back with a stick. Again, that would be me. He was as shocked as we were when he saw what had become of his inventory. His hopes and aspirations had vanished along with the dope. In a rage, he sent me packin' but not before I successfully made my case for some gas money and a healthy hit for the road. My tenure as assistant director of marketing ended as abruptly as it began. It was a good job while it lasted.

I never saw either of them again, but word on the street was he gave up on the kingpin business and put his eggs in the fortified wine tasting basket. Ruth's heart finally broke from a cocaine overdose. Although she looked much older, she was only twenty-nine years when she died.

Chapter 32
The One that Got Away

When I did my state bit, I'd hear a lot of stories about big money heists that produced cash flowing like a river. That was not my experience. Trickling like a teardrop was a more accurate description.

Bank robbery was getting to be like going to the buffet table and loading up on a half stick of celery. A thousand here, $1,500 there, and so on. How can one get by? Thinking this over, I decided I would take Mahatma Gandhi's advice and "be the change you wish to see in the world." The change I wanted: dollars.

This particular bank, a credit union to be factual, was located on lower Queen Anne Hill. According to bank-robber lore, this was the fertile land where the big money grew. I decided it was harvest time.

I'd scoped my route beforehand and my trusty chauffeur, Billy Jibs, was waiting in his Brown Bomber, a smoking, sputtering, leaking, dented hulk of an alcoholic's car. The Bomber perpetually ran out of gas, which is not an ideal situation to be in during bank robberies, so we kept a quart jar of spare fuel in the trunk for emergencies. Jibs, a Brooklyn transplant, was a heroin addict of the highest order. He weighed in at about 125, about ten pounds lighter than me. Between the two of us we made one person.

Before becoming a getaway car, this beat-up Maverick used to do a semi-honest day's work. With a sheet of plywood tied to the roof and ten or so metal garbage cans roped together, lashed to the top, it was a serviceable faux truck for hauling. More than once Jibs and I scoured neighborhoods for possible odd jobs, using our hungry appearance and a tale of woe to tap into the kindness of others, as well as their pocketbooks. It proved to be too much work for the thousand-pound gorilla of addiction we toted around. So, the Maverick became a getaway vehicle. Needing a little heroin to calm me down, I injected my liquid cajones and headed on into the credit union.

I may have been an eyesore to the teller, but I was a polite eyesore. My moniker ended up being "the Gentleman Bank Robber." After my customary "please" and "thank you," I hit the door thinking of the Venture's hit song "Walk, Don't Run." I was pleasantly surprised to find myself holding a large 3-mm thick Hefty brand trash bag full of cash, ironically the same bags I use on my construction sites today. Bless the teller's heart for providing such a sturdy bag for stuffing full of cash. The combination of my Keith Richards-style diet and its resulting muscle atrophy led me to believe that the impressive weight of the stacks of bills inside equaled triple sevens. I believed I had hit the jackpot.

The wind dropped out of my sails about three seconds out the bank door. Damned if that red smoke doesn't sting when it hits your eyes. A dreaded dye pack, the banker's safeguard, had been tossed into the bag along with the money. The plastic bag melted from the toxic chemical smoke and banded stacks of cash hit the street.

There was quite a buzz from the Queen Anne afternoon shopping crowd, not to mention the construction workers screaming and jabbing their fingers at me from scaffolding above. My ears were ringing, and I could see their lips flapping. I could have easily filled in the dialog. Like a dog's ass, I knew I was licked and had to let my prospects go. I arrived at the Brown Bomber empty handed where Jibs stood at attention, patiently waiting. I was shocked at the sight of him. He looked lost inside his oversized wardrobe.

I considered buying him a sandwich.

Though it had been only minutes, it seemed the heroin was wearing off and melancholia setting in. I wondered, was it 60K or 70K or more in red-stained bills I had left behind. My imagination and bowels ran wild. I quickly regrouped and studied my list of other potential lending institutions hoping for a better return on the dollar.

Undaunted and with the Brown Bomber practically on auto pilot, Jibs and I went straight to a less promising bank in a downtrodden neighborhood, taking it down for a whopping three hundred dollars. The teller, with head down and filing her nails, clucked her tongue and asked, "You want I should throw in the change, too?"

I said please and thank you and thought what the hell, you never know when you're going to have to feed a meter. If I hadn't been so dehydrated from all the drugs and my tear ducts had been fully functional, I believe I'd have shed a tear.

I could never quite shake the notion that if I had enough dope everything would be O.K. My whole identity was wrapped up in that thought. It was the only time I felt important. Oh, how I craved attention, and that hasn't changed. I wanted people to see the real me and to be understood though I had no idea who or what that looked like. The dregs I ran with saw me wearing a sandwich board that read "free hits of dope, as much as you want," so long as they nodded every once in a while commiserating before I overdosed.

It proved unsustainable.

Chapter 33
Special Needs

Gary lived with his special needs Mom but her needs weren't getting met. Gary had his own special needs, which rendered him totally useless as his mother's caregiver. He was stuck in between jobs, meals, girlfriends, clean clothes, hits of dope, or any coherent thought. He didn't even make it to the grocery to spend those food stamps that came once a month in the mail. This wasn't new. He had been that way for years. I knew many in his state, myself included.

What was once a respectable one story with a basement had gone to shit, one procrastinated repair at a time. His mother's house had become one of West Seattle's most dependably infested shooting galleries. Gary kept it open 24/7 forever waiting for the elusive crumb to be thrown his way. He had fierce competition as Toxic Stu's was just over snake hill. He existed in an agitated state of want. He would stand on the sagging porch like a lifeguard who looked for drowning swimmers to guide in safely. We would reward him just enough to keep him at his post. His vigilant need prevented him from going upstairs to attend to the ever-present scream of *"Gary"* that emanated through the floorboards. It was the nerve-wracking soundtrack to his fragile life. Gary was in his forties and had been stuck in that basement his whole sad life. Upstairs seemed a world away. There were rumors that there was a bathroom up there but based on the north- and south-bound traffic and the stench, the backyard seemed to be the place to go. He had been deemed incapable of work by the Social Security Administration and received a small monthly disability stipend, which barely passed through his shaky fingers before landing in the pockets of the dope man. He provided vacancy and privacy to the homeless junky at a discounted rate.

Unlike Toxic Stu, he had no cleaning requirements. The neighbors quit being an issue after the foliage was so thick and high that a path had to be carved out in order to drive into the backyard. For many a vehicle, it was a one-way trip. Quite the pile of rusted hooptie carcasses littered the yard. It was, what I imagine, hell to be like: a jungle in the middle of the city.

Gary rarely spoke. He looked at me and without words said through the years of worry carved into his forehead, "I hate my life, but it is necessary and I will live it until I expire, because that's what we junkies do."

And I wordlessly said back to him "I hate mine more, and I'm right there with you" as I did my dirty deed and handed over the syringe and half empty spoon.

I was a terrible shot. I couldn't hit a vein to save my life, which in reality probably did. My veins are what are called jumpers. The first shot would go smoothly, but after that it was like they were trying to avoid me. The harder I hit the vein, the more they moved around, and the more they moved around the harder I hit. This resulted in my arms being black and blue. They came to resemble raw hamburger. No matter the weather, I was always in need of a long sleeved shirt. When I started favoring the carotid artery, it was bring on the turtlenecks.

I would always have to enlist someone to help me as my junkie assistant—for a fee of course—someone who would gladly help me fish in order to take my stash. The alternative: me alone with a bag of useless dope that would be transformed into blood clots that hung from a filthy bathroom ceiling shot out of my plugged up syringe.

The next hit of dope was the only thing in my narrow field of vision. Food or hygiene didn't matter, the threat of arrest didn't matter and infectious disease apparently didn't matter to me either. Though my intentions were not to share needles, if it came down to a hit of dope and a dirty needle or none at all, the needle won out every time.

At ten years sober, I got a blood test that showed that I had been infected with the Hepatitis C virus. I thought there had been a mistake seeing as how it had been ten years since I had used. The virus didn't stop just because I did. I'm one of the lucky ones. The Roche Pharmaceutical Company used me as a test client for Interferon and Ribavirin combination therapy, essentially a year of chemotherapy. But now my levels are slightly higher, still, I feel good.

The occurrence of foreign matter in my blood stream was not uncommon, which occasionally resulted in fever like symptoms. Cotton fever is another risk of the afflicted I.V. drug users when they filter dope through a piece of cotton or fiberglass cigarette filter. I got it when I had to resort to what's called pounding cottons. This involves the collection of cottons from a multitude of junkies' spoons. Shooting gallery situations were the most lucrative, just add water, then draw it up into a syringe and inject. Think second pressing of olive oil.

The real danger I saw time and again was an abscess, an open sore from shooting dope over and over in one spot. When all delivery systems fail the unthinkable becomes thinkable. I accompanied one of my gallery mates to the E.R. to deal with an abscess from shooting dope between her toes.

"When I was barefoot, I stubbed my toe on a dirty syringe," she told the nurse with a straight face.

Even Dr. Willie Lump Lump wasn't buying it. I can think of a couple of people who wouldn't go to the doctor for fear of missing out on a free hit of dope. After I got arrested I found out that Billy Jeeves, who had driven in ten bank robberies for me, had a leg amputated due to abscess from shooting dope into his femur vein. He was sentenced to life without a leg. My sentence was much lighter.

Fishing is not a term just associated with the great outdoors. In junkie speak, it means overdosing on either cocaine or meth, hitting the ground and flopping like a fish out of water while your internal electrical system goes haywire. Often it's fatal, though sometimes not. In one instance, I was at a shooting gallery and this individual fished real bad. All the noble junkies but me ran out the door for help never to be seen again. Knowing C.P.R., I restarted his heart and administered mouth-to-mouth (Yuk, it's as bad as it sounds). It brought me back to reality real quick, but a half an hour later all either of us could think about was more.

Chapter 34
End of Days

I enjoy an intelligent word game as much as anyone, so what better way to pass the mind- numbingly, slow-ticking clock of county lockdown than a friendly game of Scrabble. My opponent, Psychotic Ass Wipe Man, had been brought back to King County Jail to answer for a crime of violence against another inmate while he was staying in the cozy digs of Walla Walla Penitentiary, time that would be tacked on to his already fourteen-year sentence. He probably wasn't paying attention during mandatory anger management classes.

My scrabble buddy seemed like a reasonable guy as we started our game of vocabulary skill. All was going well. We were neck and neck, right up until I played the word "jackals," a triple-word score with a fifty-point bonus, for 160 points while flapping my spasmodic jibs. Next thing I knew we were no longer neck and neck but fist and face. It was a good news/bad news kind of melee.

The bad news: P.A.W. Man had the added benefit of lifting weights on the Walla Walla iron pile, as well as about seventy pounds and four inches on me. The good news: The tables in county lock up are bolted to the floor so they can't be used as weapons, the chairs as well. Thank God. More bad news: He had plenty of arsenal in his fists. When he hit me square between the eyes, my nose took a left turn.

I was no longer the jackal. I had become the raccoon.

My knees hit the bottom of the table and this involuntarily stood me up. When in doubt, act as if. Unable to see, I flailed and landed a solid haymaker. It felt good. Seems Ass Wipe's teeth were not his own, they were on loan from the bridge society. I burned my last bridge by inadvertently sending them skittering across the nasty concrete floor. He burned me with several more blows to my brain.

After gladiator school let out, I got my atta boys from the other inmates for entertainment services rendered. I managed to slither out to the recreation yard with the other inmates unnoticed by "The Man."

Later when questioned, I feigned basketball injury by running into a concrete pillar, bullshit nobody bought that went down in the official record nevertheless. I did him "a solid" by not ratting him out. Back at the cellblock, he wanted to be my new best friend for standing up and throwing down. He felt we had done some male bonding and made a connection.

Not buying my story, the guards took me for a C.A.T. scan and on to a different cellblock. My diagnosis was chronic flapping of the jibs. Mr. Personality Disorder would have the glacially slow wait to see the prison dentist. In the spirit of Saint Francis, I prayed that he got what I most wanted for myself, corn on the cob.

I had been to that place a couple of times where I thought life or death could have gone either way. Only much, much later, after some time sober and back among the living could I appreciate how insane I had become. I am blessed to be alive. I'm in what I call my bonus years. Everything beyond the age of thirty I consider extraordinary based on my behaviors and the situations that I put myself in.

I never wanted to drag my family into the madness of my addiction. My modus operandi was just to disappear. After becoming unemployable, I had stopped coming around my mother asking for cigarettes and money to service my addiction. I knew the department stores and banks would provide. I wasn't afraid of jail; I raised my hand. It had become a place for me to crash and get right before going back out and hitting it hard.

Mom and I had a routine. I would call collect once safe in county lockup. Not willing to incur one more of my expenses, she would decline my call, relieved with the knowledge I was still alive. I would follow this up with a letter and tell her not to worry. I'd write all about how this time it would be different.

Our lockup routine continued until the day came that she accepted my call. I knew something besides me was terribly wrong. Though a petite woman, Mom had been hardened by circumstance. Even through the static-filled connection I could tell this was not her usual matter-of-fact icy tone. Her voice wavered sounding frail. She told me my brother Bill was dying of AIDS. It hit me hard because one day I hoped to get to know the brother I had never known. When I told Mom I wasn't getting out, she lost both of her sons in one fell swoop. We both retreated to do our grieving alone.

Book Three
Saved by the Bars

Chapter 35

Day one – Prison two

A typical meal in county jail would consist of the all-time most disgusting and ever-present nutra-loaf, also known as punishment blocks. These all-in-one meals supposedly contained everything a person needs to stay alive, except hope. I still don't know what was in them.

If the jail Kahunas felt generous, we would get noodles and gravy over potatoes with bread pudding for desert. The four starch groups. I gorged, nevertheless. Like so many crack-heads, I had the gaunt look of a POW. The police who arrested me could have folded me up and put me in their pocket. I was sucked up.

Through a combination of starch, no exercise or sunlight and bad water I ballooned from 135 to 180 pounds. I was as pale as a ghost and covered in a rash by the end of my five months awaiting federal prison. Sucked up or puffed up, I wasn't sure which was worse. Prison never looked so good. Having done a brief stint in state prison, I had an idea of what awaited.

Upon my arrival at the start of my one-hundred-fifteen-month federal prison sentence, I got situated in the flats. The flats were a triangular shaped open area in the middle of the housing unit that contained eleven bunk beds for twenty-two inmates on the waiting list for a cell. It was also known as the fishbowl.

"Where you from, dog?" I was asked from the top-tier convict contingency.

All eyes were on me.

"Seattle," I responded.

I knew not to say too much. There was plenty of chatter as to who I was and what I was all about. I was shrinking. It was an event.

What they wanted to know was what had I done to get there and did I have any co-defendants and ... had I ratted anybody out to save my own ass. As they pressed for details, I earned a clean bill of health: a bank robber with no co-defendants. I got a nod from above, an indication that my answer was satisfactory. I blew back up into a prideful balloon and made my way out to the big yard on a line movement to and from the cellblocks that occurred every hour.

I was happy to be away from the concrete claustrophobic confines of county jail where dominos slammed on wood tables reverberated through my head, away from where criminals not yet sentenced paced back and forth mumbling to themselves, away from where "I don't give a fuck" ruled the day, away from where Menudo was a kitchen staple, away from where an inmate said to me, "I eats the shit outa that shit," and away from where I replied, "I have no doubt."

It was summer and the stress of what King County jail had to offer, in all its iterations, was behind me. It was pleasant, despite the minor detail of the razor-wire fence and guards with shotguns to consider. After the drudgery of jail, prison was a relief. I felt almost free. I plopped myself down, along with my extra forty pounds of starch while wedged into my temporary pumpkin suit. I was wracked from being chained hands and feet to fifteen other bloated, smelly dudes in a bus for four hours on the way down. I had not yet been to the laundry for a proper set of prison attire. While the other stylish inmates wore olive khakis and brogan boots, I still wore the county scrubs that screamed fish to an ocean of sharks. I convinced myself nobody noticed me. I needed just to chill out and take it all in.

"You know you ain't gotta be wearin' that stupid shit dog?"

This helpful information was offered for free, three or four times within the span of ten minutes in my new found dog-park. So much for not being noticed.

The beach was a strip of the big yard exclusive to the white boy convicts who worked on their tans and showed off their guns, slang for biceps. I was practically translucent right about then and fit right in though it would be quite some time before I could unholster my set of guns. I watched the various cliques make plans in hushed conversation and deliver sideways glances at each other. It was apparent to me that given the opportunity many would act on their bad intentions. I watched as the guards radioed each other in anticipation, while the shotguns rode in trucks around the perimeter of the fence. I felt a little more sorry for what I had done.

Nervous energy took over. I started to pick at the grass while I surveyed my surroundings. Soon my fidgeting morphed into digging in the dirt until I grabbed the end of cold steel, an unexpected surprise. I slid it up and out of its hidey-hole while taking a quick look around to see if anyone else saw me. I deemed the coast clear and re-inserted it into the earth from where it came, where this homemade shank had been placed until the day that something jumped off, and if called upon, would inflict serious damage. I got the feeling that this shank was not alone. The relief I'd felt just moments earlier melted away. It dawned on me my one-hundred-fifteen-month sentence would take damn near ten years to complete.

It's a mystery where this extra steel would have come from. As I later discovered, everything is meticulously accounted for in prison. The guards would periodically lock us down in our cells doing a sweep of the yard with metal detectors meting out collective punishment for weapons found. The rats would then come forward, give up a name or two and nibble on some cheese in the form of favorable treatment. With lockdown over and the losers carted off to the prison within the prison, the game would start all over again—steel stolen, new shanks made, new hiding spots put to use—as it has been played since the first convict spent the first day in the first prison.

Chapter 36
A Crushing Blow

Upon my arrival to the cellblock, I settled in on the flats, which was like a sunken living room. I was on view for all to see. Crusher was sent on a mission to confirm who I was and why I was there, a process that often occurs in the early stages of baptism to prison life. I knew the deal, the usual purpose being to glean information about my crime, financial status and so on. Crusher asked me a few questions and shared with me that he too was a mediocre bank robber and a great drug addict.

"Come with me, you're one of us," he said.

Oh, fuck not already, I thought.

I'd heard the stories. Thankfully this wasn't a booty call. It turns out Crusher was sober and initiated me into the sober ranks as well. We became fast friends and stayed that way until the wheels came off his precarious wagon. I stayed sober, he didn't. It often works that way.

Being a Seattle bank robber, I was always on the lookout for other Seattle bank robbers. Kindred spirits and all that shit. Enter Red. Red played the drums; I played the drums. Red robbed banks, I robbed banks. Red didn't want to be sober; I wanted to be sober.

I bludgeoned him with recovery material from above and talked incessantly about the virtues of not drinking and using. He wasn't having any of it. The sole focus of his existence was to get loaded. He got a job in the bakery and lasted about two days before he got sacked for stealing an overabundance of yeast. Off to the hole he went for thirty days. As hard as I tried, I couldn't make him me. I believed that I had failed at my job, I took it personally and came on down from my mighty mentor throne.

Red arrived at a place where he felt it necessary to make a knife out of a melted toothbrush and a Gillette Track Two for a closer shave. None of this weenie wrist cutting business for Red, he knew how to get-er-done. He cut himself under the armpit while locked in his cell in the middle of the night, very effective, a river of Red.

Kenny, Red's cellmate was a champion of the pill line and heavily sedated. Until the effects of his meds wore off, he was totally oblivious to the fact that blood had dripped down through the mattress of the top bunk and saturated him. He ran in place and struggled to gain traction in what he momentarily thought was his own pool of blood. Kenny flapped his arms and screamed bloody murder in his shrill medicated voice. The guards took Red out of their cell and left Kenny alone in his attempt to take flight. Kenny took a shower and some more sedatives instead. I caught a glimpse of the carnage and noticed Red had written "DETH" on the wall in large letters and all caps. I figured he knew he was about to run out of blood, expedited things and skipped the A.

Miracle of miracles, Red lived. After a year of psychiatric evaluation at the Springfield Missouri medical unit, he was back and manic as ever. He and Crusher became best fast friends. I kept a little distance.

Since Crusher's cellmate was a big dog in the heroin trade and sold dope for the Columbians, Crusher could not consider his cell a safe house. As the guards rolled up on their cell, and Crusher flushed the dope down the toilet, Crusher, and his cellie now owed the Columbians, never a good position to be in.

The Columbians said they'd squash the debt if Crusher put a little scare into a Mexican the Columbians felt was encroaching on their turf. Crusher enlisted Red, the problem solver. They went a little overboard and put him in a vegetative state. It wasn't supposed to go down like that.

The rumor mill churned. The F.B.I. took about four minutes to lock down the prison yard and identify the responsible parties because of a laundry bag. This particular bag was bloody and in the washer with inmate I.D. name and number on it. It was used to wrap the heavy object that did the damage. The laundry bag belonged to one or another of the perpetrators. Not the most well thought out plan.

I never saw Red or Crusher again, although I know they each received a heavy addition to their already stiff sentences. After an extended lockdown, the ensuing gang riot between the Mexicans and the Columbians transpired. All fifty or so Columbians were taken off the yard and dispersed throughout the Federal prison system.

Not all Escobar's are bad guys by my calculations. Pablo's cousin Alex administered C.P.R. and saved the life of one of my friends who was having a heart attack, which was an eye-opener for me.

Observing Red and Crusher helped bolster my recovery program. I've recently been in contact with Crusher through the miracles of social media. He is out, sober and has turned his life around. Red is still a gray area.

Chapter 37
Commissary

Every ten days or so, my housing unit's turn to go shopping arrived in the prison rotation. This much-anticipated event was a bright star on the black hole of our existence; we viewed it as the single most important event in our monotonous prison life—with the exception of release. Most products for sale came from Keefe Supply Company, a lowbrow food, and toiletries manufacturer that makes everything look unappealing, because, what're we going to do, go somewhere else? Keefe specialized in super toxic Dow-style chemical cheese spooge, esophagus burning instant coffee crystals and skin stripper bath soap, to name a few. This company commits their crimes exclusively against their captive convict consumers.

For many, shopping was the opportunity to pay off those weekly gambling debts from college football, baseball, shuffleboard, loogy-toss, whatever, it didn't matter. Gambling fever ran high in prison. Convicts would gamble on anything. You could tell who had lost big by their overstuffed laundry bags full of high-ticket items, such as shoes, sweat pants and cartons of cigarettes to be paid out to the bookies. As a courtesy, the bookies often provided a free escort service—I call them *The Lights of Reason*—paid thugs who made those with a history of getting lost find their way back with the goods. The losers sported their upside down smiles as they moped back down the lonely trail to their perspective housing units purged of their pitiful paychecks. Yours truly was excluded, perhaps the first sign my newfound sobriety also came with newfound sanity. Gambling was never my thing. I got my money's worth from the entertainment value of watching from afar.

I looked forward to sampling some of the over- priced offerings available in our one-store town. When the guards called commissary over the PA system and the doors to our housing units opened, a stampede ensued. Think Walmart on Black Friday... with convicts. Only the announcement for psych meds proved more dangerous.

The commissary store had limited shelf space, and with all the excessive purchasing going on, it was a good motivator for me to get in shape in preparation for the fight for a decent spot in line. Entrepreneurial inmates sold places in line as well.

Inmates were not allowed to run unless actually on the outdoor running track, so this migration to the commissary resembled Olympic speed walking. Being a veteran of running from the police made a smooth transition to speed walking. I consistently positioned myself in a respectable spot in the line. I would quickly present my prison ID card, number 07384-085 (once given a prison number, one never forgets it), to the inmate clerk for funds verification. Then I'd hand over my filled-out commissary list and wait to be called. Once called, from the opposite side of a metal grate they'd stuff my goods into a metal drawer that resembled a drive-up bank teller window as I would simultaneously unload. The transfer often resulted in mutilation, such as potato chip dust. It was a laborious process, indeed.

Ben and Jerry's ice cream was "the shit" (translation: very popular). There was a buzz about their new flavor, White Russian. With pictures of mustachioed Cossacks kicking up their heels, arms folded, clad in furry hats, I must say, it did look rather attractive, so I made an impulse buy. Out on the yard, as I prepared to dig into "this shit" I checked the White Russian label. I'm an avid label reader, and I noticed that in this ice cream's ingredient list, appearing right after the carrageenan, was the word "Kahlua." A whiff of sadness hit me followed by a trickle of generosity as I gave my pint to Vino Vinnie. I knew it was "none for me, thanks." I'm allergic to alcohol; every time I drink, I break out in handcuffs.

Previous shoppers sparked the word that blazed through the dry weeds of prison gossip. Guys were soon cramming their laundry bags full with pints of Ben and Jerry's White

Russian ice cream. This multitude of numbskulls intended to get their buzz on one lick at a time. Now I'm no mathematician, but my quick tally indicated that it would take somewhere in the neighborhood of eight pints an hour to get even a mild buzz if one could avoid cardiac arrest before arrival. Nevertheless, in tribute to tenacity, some gave inebriation by ice cream their best college dropout try. Instead of relief from their problems with a warm glow, they became sick as dogs and in worse mental shape than when they had begun.

Courtesy of a khaki-wearing fly on the wall, the prison officials pulled the plug on this nonsensical endeavor shortly after it started. Not because they thought these guys would succeed in their quest to become alcoholic stupor-stars, but rather because they didn't want to deal with the ramifications of en masse diabetic comas.

Inmate stores—all unsanctioned—were popular for cravings between commissary visits. Every housing unit had at least a couple of inmate loan shark mercantiles. As a business model, similar to Moneytree. In prison, it's called "Two for Threes." A person could borrow two items in exchange for three items paid back the following week. If the debt was not paid, the price doubled each week. What was once a $20 debt could become hundreds of dollars of debt in short order with the bonus of bodily harm thrown in for free.

Chapter 38
Body Armor

A serious meth epidemic broke out inside during the first year of my federal prison sentence. Convicts were running off the rails. I can think of nothing worse than being all jacked up on meth locked in a small cage with another wild animal that would become the focus of paranoia. "Do I need to eliminate this imaginary threat?"

I had the foresight to screen my cellmates to ensure I cohabited with only the highest quality degenerate who like myself didn't partake in the toxic brew of battery acid, toluene, crushed up sulfur from match heads, cold tablets and the like.

I got to watch the madness rather than participate in it for a change. Quite refreshing.

The housing units were configured in a triangle. Thirty cells on the top tier, thirty on the bottom, all two-man cells looking out onto the flats, the homeless prison encampment. A total of 140 inmates give or take a few, with a corridor that connected the A-side mirroring the B-side. Four identical units. Total prison population twelve hundred including The Hole. The housing units were built for visibility, so that when something "jumped off," all could see. There were no bad seats.

During said epidemic, one particularly spun-out junkie abandoned his cell with a war cry ready to do battle wearing nothing but a suit of body armor he had fashioned out of *National Geographic* magazines. He may have gotten the idea from the magazines themselves, ancient warriors chewing coca leaves wearing stone tablets with inscriptions. It was totally functional. If he had been in a real battle, I doubt the swords could penetrate. On that day, the battle only raged between his ears until he drew the attention of the guards. Then he got his fight and did evade the authorities' clutches for a time. The guards eventually neutralized him. He got hog-tied with feet and hands behind his back and carried away like a verbally abusive suitcase. The cellblock got locked down and tossed for drugs. Everyone had something to talk about for a while, and I gave thanks that I only wanted *National Geographic* for reading.

This wasn't the only naked confrontation with guards that occurred. There was the occasional in-the-buff inmate greased head-to-toe with Vaseline and whacked on meth who invited the guards into his cell for an ass whoopin'. The guards took their lumps while trying to get a hold of the naked Superman like a pig at a fair. Plan B was the fire hose. A good long blast up against his cell wall took the fight right out of him. Then it was off to The Hole and pill line to rest up so he could come back out and fight the good fight again.

Nobody caused more concern for guards and inmates alike than the Marielitos from Cuba. In 1980, Castro put them on a boat and shoved them towards Miami. What to do with them? This question defied answers. After being arrested for a minor infraction such as public inebriation, they would go to a local jail. From there Immigration and Naturalization services would transfer them into the hungry mouth of the federal prison system. They were charged with no crime and possessed no release date. Yes, I'm talking about the United States. Most started their time at the United States Prison in Atlanta, where they promptly took scores of guards hostage and burned down a portion of the prison. If I was made to get on a boat to a foreign country by my crazy dictator president, then got rounded up and locked away for what could be forever by a crazy movie actor turned president, I might have a little arson in me as well.

After the Atlanta debacle, they were dispersed throughout the system, so their numbers were less concentrated. In theory, they'd be more easily manageable. They settled into a life of uncertainty. There were no advocates, no family, no parole board, really nothing to look forward to, no hope. I knew and worked with many, and not all were Scarface. Some, in my opinion, were decent human beings. But, a decade or more in lockup without a hearing made many act out. One Cuban inmate who worked with me had Revelations tattooed all over his face, damn near the whole chapter. He had a habit of throwing shit at the guards followed by a trip to The Hole and would then do it all over again every couple of months when he got out. This is how he did his time, and it went on for years. The other inmates felt empathy and knew he and his compatriots were capable of being dangerous.

Nobody fucked with the Cubans.

Chapter 39

Switzerland

I'm not a joiner. I've always been skeptical of joining anything, although Ill Will did buy me a one-year membership to the Loyal Order of Moose in Alaska for my eighteenth birthday. I never did get a chance to drink with the other Bulls. I wasn't interested in their secret handshake or praying to the God of libation. I would later become a member of the West Seattle Weasel Lodge.

One of the first cons in prison is convincing first-timers that they need to "join"—click up, as it's called in prison slang—a gang or tribe of some sort as a matter of protection and power. I'm a bald white guy. That doesn't mean I'm a Neo-Nazi or a Skinhead, it only means I'm a bald white guy. And according to my experience one doesn't have to join anything in prison. I didn't require protection because I wasn't into the drama. I had the advantage of being a little bit older, and not so good looking. I had done state time, so I wasn't totally freaked out. Still, as a bald white guy, many decided I was a natural for the bald white guy clique of the Neo-Nazis or Skinheads. I was approached and given the dumbass redneck test and failed miserably according to the curriculum. It removed any doubt I would join. From there I was free to go about the business of doing my time.

League sports were a big deal in the joint and about the only thing I did join. For me, it was softball, fast pitch and slow pitch. Each spring as many as eighteen teams competed for glory. There was an "A" league and a "B" league, so nobody was excluded who had a desire to play. This was the only time in prison when there were rules, and it was relatively safe. Umpires studied the rule-books, and we all took it seriously. I started in "B" league and moved up to "A" after honing my skills.

For the elderly or more laid back there was Bocce Ball or Shuffleboard. The Columbians had a pro-caliber soccer team before their demise. There was also flag football, world-class handball players, basketball and my favorite to watch, field hockey. Because I worked in special projects in the mill as a woodworker, I got to make the hockey sticks.

The inmates didn't play field hockey on a field. They played on the gym floor on self-segregated teams that amounted to little more than organized race riots. No rules, Total mayhem. The walking track above the gym offered a great vantage point to watch the participants whack the bejabbers out of each other with sticks of maple. I took great pride in my craftsmanship. In the end, field hockey didn't work out. Too many fights that spilled out beyond the gym floor, and the plug was finally pulled.

Basketball offered its own version of contact sport. On the court, Guy was a one-man wrecking ball and not your standard package as far as basketball players went. Five-foot ten and close to three hundred pounds, he humored me in games of one-on-one so I could get a serious cardio workout. He had Steve Nash handling skills and rarely missed the net.

He was Native American and played on the Indian team. The blacks had a great team too, but Guy's big stomach always dashed their dreams. He would throw down 60 points from behind his head. Indefensible. He would laugh and laugh as the opposing team would become unraveled and fight amongst themselves.

Chapter 40
Foreign Correspondent

"She's going to want to know me, and then, in ten years when I get out, we can build a life together." That was the lonely inmate's thin thread of lustful thinking as they invested in the *Foreign Female for Correspondence Magazine*.

This publication promised domestic bliss, mostly in the form of Russian women seeking prosperous American husbands. I wasn't so sure that being broke and in prison could be counted in that category. Many though refused to be dissuaded.

Magazines of this type all had the same pitch: Just send in your substantial subscription fee, pick your international poison, and voila! "Instant fauxmance." The magazine filled its not-so-glossy, second-rate, printed pages with vintage Russian photos of foxy comrades like Svetlana, Natalia, and Olga who would send back promising, flowery, cookie-cutter letters, which, in reality, were likely written by the meaty paws of Igor, Yuri, and Boris.

It was a two-way scam. These lonely inmates labored day and night in the furniture factory for less than a dollar an hour to send away their hard earned pennies and perpetuate a lie that would never see the light of day. What was the stated purpose of these female correspondents' requests for much-needed rubles? It was to pay for the upcoming American-Russian wedding.

My cellie was one of the afflicted.

"What should I tell her I do?" he asked me.

"You mean him," I said.

"Shut the fuck up."

"Tell her you're a rocket scientist. They love that kind of shit in Russia. Or better yet, tell her you work at the Federal Reserve printing money."

After sending off the last of his cash and awaiting one more letter that would never come, my cellie was the clear loser in this battle of the scammers and discovered that his true love's inkwell had run dry in tandem with his money well. Snapped back into reality to recover from his snakebite, he realized the error of his ways and focused his attentions on another inmate's sister.

Mail-Order Brides are big business on the outside, too. Of course, there's a slightly better chance for a successful outcome. I have an acquaintance that arranged for a Chinese wife. She, however, isn't the first woman he paid a bride-price to obtain. I think the first one may have been defective because she disappeared with a substantial amount of his personal assets. This second time around he must have negotiated a package deal because it looks like he got some free uncles, brothers and cousins thrown in as well. All in all, it appears to be a happy enough marriage for all ten of them.

E.E.

Chapter 41
The Smut Wrangler

Our new warden, Mr. Antiseptic, was hired with the task of giving the joint a complete pornographic scrub down. He was a man who considered the kneecaps of a Nun to be too risqué. He had his minions confiscate all incoming literary masterpieces such as *Booty Patrol* and *Gap* magazines that had been lovingly sent by the inmates' family members for their viewing pleasure through the U.S. mail. This action put a serious dent in the prison porn coffers and created a wide-open black market.

Cowboy was the resident smut wrangler at our Dude Ranch. The role that suited him well, seeing as he claimed to be a former pimp. I don't know if he actually rode a horse or roped steers back in Compton, California from where he came, but he did let us know that he once had a stable of fillies. Forced into wearing brogans (ugly prison boots) and khakis like the rest of us, it is possible he would need serious fashion reintegration once he returned to his homies on the range.

With the lecherous trench coat element jockeying for position, Cowboy rode to the top and became just the hombre to fill the void. He sewed pockets into the lining of his coat, one above the other, fashioning a nifty magazine display rack for easy window-shopping and distribution. Cowboy would show up at a predetermined location with his mobile literary red-light district and spread his coat open like a pair of wings. His patrons chose from what appeared to be a half-naked female choir. Cowboy was the librarian matchmaker, allowing these cell warriors to engage in some serious hand-to-penis combat once back to their confines.

Cowboy's literary fillies required a safe-house, somewhere they would be comfortable cooling their heels while waiting for their next gig. They were constantly being moved around to avoid detection from the roving eyes of the non-paying goon squad. Like fine art in a museum, upon return, these pieces were carefully examined, cataloging all identifying marks. Any new stains introduced to the artwork would levy serious fines. Cowboy, the curator, and his team of art security enforcers, the XXX men, would see to that. Cowboy ran a smooth operation. It was no secret who the hardcore patrons were. This knowledge came in handy when figuring out whose hands to avoid shaking. With a good chance that Cowboy himself was the D.N.A. train central station, I gave him a wide berth, as well.

Some guards on the cellblock let the comings and goings of the smut wrangler slide to some extent, but they were also required to toss an occasional cell and produce some X-rated contraband to keep the Warden at bay. Less coveted rags that were battle worn and had already served their tour of duty were taken out of circulation and left out as scraps for the vulture guards to pick clean.

After all, they were in prison, too.

Chapter 42
Invasion of the Booty Snatchers

My first year in prison was also my first year in recovery. During a meeting, it was suggested that I not get into an intimate relation within my first year so I wouldn't upset my emotional apple cart. Considering my surroundings, I offered no objections. I took a vow of celibacy with the exception of self-service.

When I got out of prison, it seemed that every so often someone would ask me with a twinkle in their eye, "So, were there a lot of rapes in prison?"

"Not to my knowledge," I'd say.

"Was it hard?" they would ask.

"It was never hard," I would say.

Gay sex was the elephant in the prison living room. The joint teemed with homo *faux* bics who made a grand show of their uber manliness while getting busy behind cell doors.

No one in prison is gay. Sex was referred to as stick pussy, and that made it a non-gay, A-OK, hetero activity. Gay for the stay. The word fag was bandied about plenty by the discreet partakers of carnal corn, who missed the irony of their intended slight. Still, no one raised the rainbow flag.

You never knew who would wind up on the short end of the Magic Johnson.

Everyone gets the safe sex talk from staff upon arrival: "Beware the hungry convict fisherman trolling for trouser trout" and, "and remember, butt piracy is a crime," and so on and so forth. Yet, there were no condoms to be found. It was literally Screw U. The predictable result of high risk and a high rate of sexually transmitted disease and H.I.V. occurred. Black market latex gloves went on sale as stand-ins for the missing condoms.

Yikes.

Things are logistically tight inside a prison, and there was no room for secrets. There were no secrets in prison, by inmates or staff. Things just weren't talked about.

Mary, formerly known as Larry, had the courage to change. She was a tranny in transition and was arrested in the midst of hormone replacement treatment. Mary still sported a little stubble on the chin but was generously endowed upstairs. She hoped to finish her time in a women's institution one day. I learned this in the band room where Mary picked the piano back up after a time. It didn't matter that she had a red heart sewn on the back of her gym shorts, my band-mates and I were glad to have her.

As I had learned as a kid, being a drummer is a great way to beat the shit out of something and only get into a little trouble, usually related to timing. My band, The Poor Dumb Bastards, rocked the yard. Our lead singer Yoker farted so bad while we practiced that we made him run his mic cord under the door and sing from outside the band room.

Riley dreamed of being sober. He'd been selling the only thing he had to support his drug habit, his ass. My sober cohorts and I helped him believe that he could quit the behaviors that led to the behaviors. We negotiated a payment plan with his creditors, who, despite what they were into, had a glimmer of respect for what he was trying to undo. One day at a time he did stay sober, tightened his sphincter and expanded his horizons.

Viagra was just making its first promotional appearance on television right before I got out. The still hard-core junkies made big plans.

"I'll crush it up and smoke it, put it on my cereal, take three or four and mix it with other drugs." Their major oversight would be no one for them to share it with and what to do in case of overdose. Call your doctor? Hell, call your nurse. Just how exactly would resuscitation work?

When I got out, I was terrified of the prospect of having sex. The only thing I knew was that it had never worked out well in the past. It was a messy and embarrassing debacle. No one inside the prison ever admitted that they too were terrified, but I've got to believe that was the case. You'd never know it with all the displaced tattooed Casanovas roaming the prison yard discussing their non-stop sexcapades.

One of my wife's girlfriends counseled me that our bodies would get to know and like each other, resulting in success. Smart woman, she was correct. I didn't end up needing Viagra though I did try it once with my then-girlfriend and now wife. We spent more time washing sheets than anything else. It turns out my low self-image was occupying the world's biggest bullshit factory housed between my ears.

Piotter 194

Chapter 43

The Worm and Cool Hand Luke

❝❝I could do that, it ain't no big deal," the Worm said after watching *Cool Hand Luke* on the cellblock TV.

Cool Hand Luke was an institution in our institution, a cinematic god, and the Worm believed he could measure up. Since there were no parking meters to knock the heads off of in our prison, Worm must have been referring to Luke eating the fifty hard-boiled eggs. Worm was not this fellow's real name. It's doubtful that this was a self-assigned moniker. It certainly was not a name that struck fear into the hearts of the other inmates. I don't know if he earned it because he enjoyed digging in the dirt or feeding robins. And, of course, I'm pretty sure no one had ever yet tried to cut him in half to see if he would replicate. However he got his name, it was the name on everyone's tongue after his boast.

For this particular event, sports books were organized. Books of stamps and cigarettes were pooled for the payouts as everyone wagered whether Worm would stop at thirty eggs. Bookies set the over-under at 5-2 odds or forty eggs at 4-1. The date was set, the bets laid, and The Big Yard chosen as the obvious venue.

This Egg McNasty event had to be planned around the prison menu. It required the migration of fifty hard-boiled eggs, which came two eggs, one inmate at a time, from the chow hall. When motivated, inmates can be scary effective. The eggs were heisted without missing a beat.

The appointed day was a sunny one, word traveling fast and the Big Yard was packed. Even the most casual of sports fans came out.

"In thisss corner, Worm, weighing in at about three hundred pounds!" Fang spit out to the excited crowd. "And in thisss corner, fifty hard-boiled eggs, weighing in at about eight pounds!" He hissed through his diminished grill.

Just like in the movie, watches were synchronized and set at three minutes, and just like any serious sporting event, Doc was standing by at the ready to monitor the Worm in case of a heart attack or stroke.

Worm had put it all on the line.

Fang, who was perpetually in Worm's shadow, yelled "Chow!"

Worm attacked. He came from hearty stock. He slid one egg after another down his generous gullet with an economy of motion and as nonchalant as if he were popping M&Ms. Worm's innards knew no bounds; his tract operated with the fluidity of an efficient assembly line. He got fifteen down in thirty seconds without even chewing. O.M.F.G. Next up, four at a time chewed, he did this five times in a row. That's thirty-five down, with fifteen left and one minute to go. It looked to me like he had a pretty good system. He had been transferred from another joint and done this before.

I was sickly fascinated and an immediate fan.

Fang handed Worm one peeled egg after another, the crowd's enthusiasm reached a crescendo. Worm's guts were already processing the mighty mess, and from the smell of things I thought that both he and his cellmate Fang, might not survive the night. Ah, the fog of war.

What happened next should have been enough to trigger a chain-reaction gag reflex in the entire crowd, but we had already donated our breakfast. I did see many with hand over mouth like they were in deep prayer. You would think that under the circumstances the Worm would be the one to vomit in earnest, but not entirely so. It was obvious that he did lose a portion of his lunch, but he kept it contained within his cupped hands and what came up went back down again.

There was a momentary pause while Worm read his palms, he may have considered his mortality and thought about potential beneficiaries if he didn't make it. Snapped back into the reality that he didn't own Jack Shit, Worm turned to the task at hand and soldiered on until he had muscled down the last fifteen eggs. As the last egg disappeared into his bloated maw, he barely beat the clock and became a rock star for a day, an instant celebrity.

I don't know how many postage stamps and cigarettes exchanged hands in the aftermath, but no one who wagered on that day was too upset to pay. They considered it the mere cost of admission to the greatest show on earth, or at least on our prison's little patch of it.

Chapter 44
Thor

Everyone involved in the Wiccan sweat lodge wanted to be a Viking or already believed they came from the direct line of Odin, father of the gods. If an inmate was blessed with a red beard, a clean jacket (a list of admirable crimes that he wore into prison), and a lost soul, he could become a potential shot caller or clan leader, if you will.

The Native Americans had their own sweat lodge at the prison, so the Wiccan contingency—kind of a mixed bag of Viking bikers, skinheads, and redneck white supremacists—lobbied for and eventually received their sweat lodge. The warden caved, deciding it was easier to allow for freedom of religion and all that nonsense.

All the misguided whiteys that queued up to be honorary Vikings proved to be a boon for the resident Skinhead tattoo artist. With his makeshift tat gun, he would ink intricate Norse designs and an array of shockingly racist themes. Some were in need of new limbs for lack of real estate. The lodge members' demands enabled him to live large in a very small way for the remainder of his prison sentence.

The Viking industry proved to be lucrative for me as well. Working in the special projects section of the prison furniture factory, I was the go-to-guy when it came to the manufacturing of miniature Thor's magical hammer pendants, which were to be worn around the Nordic necks on a piece of macramé string. This added some lackluster bling for this group that I referred to as the Thor-skins. The pendant was a required tool and necessary symbol for fighting the miniature evil spirits that emanated from the prison sweat lodge. No self-respecting Viking redneck/peckerwood/skinhead/meth-head would be caught dead without his mighty warrior's hammer. I was an equal-opportunity opportunist. I set up my miniature hammer shop on the sly, turning out enough of the mighty magical hammers to satisfy the hordes.

No one outside the hollowed circle knew what earth shattering wonderments took place in the lodge meetings; that was privileged information. But I imagined them sitting in a circle sweating, with my handcrafted hammers between thumbs and forefingers, bonking each other over their Viking heads and letting out mighty roars. For their offering to the gods, there were no animals to slaughter or sacrifice. Some secretly voted for Hebrew National hot dogs, momentarily putting their racism aside knowing that that meat was of superior quality and had already answered to a higher authority. It was decided to make do with sub-standard prison dogs, roasted on a stick over their open fire pit. This would be an acceptable second choice as voted by the Viking Council. Oh, how the mighty had fallen. WWOD! What would Odin do?

Piotter 202

.

Chapter 45
Chow

Despite the obvious lack of culinary diversity, prison food was a step up from county jail. Once a week the new menu would come out for the following week to give us a glimpse of what we had to look forward to. El Rancho Stew was nothing but the finest cuts, butts and noses, knuckles and toes. Noodles Jefferson was always a favorite. Wasn't he our second president? The five hundred pounds of liver and onions cooking all at once on a pool table sized grill brought tears to my eyes. The prison staff often gave creative license to the inmate cooks, resulting in giant vats of unrecognizable foodstuff, enough to feed twelve hundred.

I worked in the kitchen for the first thirty-nine months of my federal bit. The dish room, just like a sauna, was also a great place to make wine. Though I did not partake, my crew was half drunk half the time. I made a commitment to be the best Hydro Plastics Technician and had the cleanest dishes any joint has ever seen. It was much appreciated by inmate and staff alike.

Real killers with real knives often do the prep work. The prep rooms are enclosed behind Plexiglas. The tables are about ten feet apart and bolted to the floor. Cables were bolted to the table and knives welded to the cable. If they tried to stick each other, they'd come up a little bit short. No chance of a knife fight here.

Still, life in the kitchen was never dull. Hells Angel Rocky was a casualty of meth and bad hygiene; his teeth were long gone. When he sought me out he feared his dentures were long gone too. He knew he would lose his tough guy edge if he had to eat only mush and become the Gerber baby of his biker gang. He told me that he had left his dentures on a food tray, and they ended up within the tonnage of waste. Not expecting them to eat their way out, I strapped on my dumpster diving suit and sprang into action. I became a Hells Angel angel. I was lead man on the dish crew, and all my guys dove deep into the muck to lend a hand. Filtering through can after can of garbage seemed just like old times.

I surfaced with his crooked and decayed dentures and made my presentation. Rocky dunked them in his glass of water for a cursory rinse, wiped them under his armpit and fitted them in. He was mighty grateful as was apparent by his award-winning sinister smile. This brought some much-appreciated clout to my small world.

Word was out.

"This guy's all right, don't fuck with him."

Screw Visa. In prison, that's priceless.

Holidays were totally underwhelming. Thanksgiving especially. A big production was made to be sure, but the delivery was sorely lacking. The menu indicated all the traditional fare. Turkey with stuffing, pumpkin pie, etc. The inmate cooking staff pulled together with a bit of extra effort. I had to admit it looked and smelled good. The housing units were let out to chow on a rotating schedule. 3-B won the lottery so on this day we were first. I got my plate loaded up and sat down at my usual table when Officer Eat Shit And Die started to hustle everyone out.

"ALL RIGHT DUMP YOUR TRAYS, EVERYONE OUT, LET'S GO. LET'S GO. WE GOTTA MAKE ROOM FOR THE NEXT GROUP," he yelled to us.

After shoving some pumpkin pie down my pants, Officer Grope, who worked the door, pointed out to me that we're not allowed to take food out of the chow hall. They could have just kept us locked in our cells and thrown the food directly in the trash and cut out the middleman. That's where most of it ended up. That glitch would be remedied on later holidays. They pulled the bully guards and staffed the chow hall with real human beings disguised as guards.

One Thanksgiving, the flightless turkeys flew the coop. Twenty-seven birds escaped. The third guard in line to be the chow hall boss, known as Mr. Childless, had been narrowed down as the culprit. There was much speculation as to why he filled the expansive trunk of his car. Did he have a tryptophan addiction or maybe he sold them to needy families? All we knew is Thanksgiving would be pretty sparse.

Mr. Childless resembled Fatty Arbuckle, the silent film star, minus the comedy. Anti-hilarious, and a nasty guy to work for. He was one of the guards that longed to be a judge so he could mete out his punishment and make the prison experience as degrading as possible. And like a prisoner behaving badly, he too disappeared into the far reaches never to be seen again. After the case of the missing turkeys was uncovered, rumor had it that he was promoted to assistant food administrator at a prison in Colorado. Hopefully, Super Max underground.

Chapter 46
The Name Game

I never knew half the names of the inmates I did time with over the years, not their birth names anyway unless their parents were the guilty ones. Most everyone in prison has a nickname.

When names are considered, one must carefully consider a category. Baddest dude in the land, sidekick, smart guy, wise guy, from the hills, Mr. Big, Joker and so on. Here are few of the real fake names I interacted with: T-Bone, Too Hard, T-Money, Money, Mo Money, O.G. (meaning old gangster), B.G. (baby gangster), Dollar Bill, Billion Dollar Bill, Cha Ching, Cash Money, Mountain Man, Mountain 1, Mountain 2, Brown Man, Half a Man, Round man, Big Man, Little man, Space man, Goat man (there's always a goat man), Fat Bob and Buffer Bob (he had a wild parakeet that landed on his shoulder daily). There was no Sponge Bob. Real horses were everywhere Yellow Horse, White Horse, Red Horse, Blue Horse, Not to be confused with the fake names of guys named after just the color, like Red, Blue, Brown, Green, and Black. I knew Taz, Cuz, Scuzz, Kong, Bong (a throwback from Woodstock), Dog, Big Dog, Road

Dog, Mad Dog, Mud Dog, Gray Dog, there was no Gay Dog.

Rocks were almost as popular as horses and dogs: J Rock, G Rock, K-Rock, that's a krock, and D Rock, as in dumb as a. I also knew a Doc (a real doctor whose council I often sought), Hacksaw (didn't do him any good, he's still in), Flatch, Sleaze, Shamu, Greeze, Worm, Wheezy, Waterhead, Grateful Ned, Bear, Catfish, Gopher and Animal (though one I think must be down on the evolutionary scale due to a lack of frontal lobe formation. I liked to think of him as minimal).

My name, as crazy as it might seem, was Doug.

Then there was Batman, and he was at his perch. He claimed the forty-two-inch section of horizontal railing at the front of his cell cave. My perch was fourteen feet and three cells down. Batman was a mumbler, with low-level anger directed at no one in particular. Looking like he had bit into a lemon, he dissed out a constant cascade of slights for our listening pleasure. His acerbic worldview, nasty as you please, splattered every passerby.

"Fuck this, fuck that, fuck no, fuck off and fuck you," he would say.

This would be his daily proclamation, prison poetry.

Like a human tele-type machine, he reported and commented on all the days' events while never leaving his post. He had stamina. You could go to chow, come back and pick up the thread where you had left off. He spewed it in a loop, just like CNN. Those of us who'd been around awhile knew it was a natural part of our scenery. We looked forward to it and gave him a free pass for when it turned insulting or obnoxious, which was often in part because he was on psych meds.

Mostly, we considered it free entertainment. He was so prolific he had his greatest hits. Like the time War decided to join the Skinheads.

Young Warren, War for short, was a newbie to the tribe of Lost Whiteys. He was all set for his inaugural tattoo, a ritual to bring him into the fold. The tat would be displayed on the backs of his arms indicating what race he was currently a part of, in case anyone was wondering. He opted for the (always popular) Pecker Wood tattoo. A logical choice being two words that say, "I'm an uneducated white racist." The resident skinhead tattoo artist might have been unaware that in the good ole U.S. of A. we read left to right. Leading with "pecker" on the back of Warren's right arm, he never realized his error and motored ahead. As a freshly inked Skinhead, War set out to wow the crowd sporting his new Woodpecker tattoo. A chorus of cartoon Woody sounds started echoing through the cellblock. Batman, who missed nothing, had plenty to say.

Warren was confused. He didn't realize he had been woodpeckered.

"Hey Woody," Batman said snickering, "are you studyin' to be an ornithologist?"

Warren's blood boiled from the paired embarrassment of being clowned and his ignorance of bird science. Batman and Woodpecker were soon locked in a convict embrace of the non-spooning variety. It would be the second bad thing that happened to War that day. Turns out Batman, a Vietnam vet, had superhero tendencies. He got the better of young Warren by twisting him up into a pretzel. Up until then Warren considered him to be nothing more than a loud-mouthed, feeble old man. The Goon Squad arrived and carted them off for their prospective months in The Hole.

Without Batman, we were forced to suffer the day's events uninformed, and without War we would have to settle for peace.

Chapter 47
Lockdown

When something is about to jump off, everybody knows it. A buzz of negative energy hangs in the air. A mad scramble in the housing unit would take place to prepare for the inevitable lockdown that follows such prison hijinks.

First on the agenda: get my dirty clothes into the washing machine and worry about drying them later. Take a shower, because I never knew when my next shower would be. Let my cellmate have a little personal time in the cell for personal business. Get me some books. Wheel and deal for cigarettes or any other creature comforts available, and fast. Settle into my twenty-six-inch wide by seventy-two-inch long cookie sheet bunk and two-inch-thick, fireproof plastic-covered mattress and expend as little energy as possible. Sleep and read often, try to become a character in my book.

Eight days was my longest lockdown with four or five not uncommon.

When a prison is locked down, it's as it sounds. You don't leave your cell. You eat the same bagged meal for breakfast, lunch and dinner. Bologna sandwiches for breakfast, lunch and dinner. That's a whole lot of baloney. You can't make calls or exercise. You stay in your cell.

Seasoned veterans stayed quiet. Newbies and pill liners often cracked. They'd yell and scream until the goon squad came to extract them. Their lockdowns would become extended stays elsewhere, in The Hole or the hospital or some version of both. There would always be an end to it and then back to the daily madness of what I considered my normal routine. The madness was never far away.

Like Tommy's coat. Tommy, an aging biker who long ago lost his mojo had a coat that was pure madness: hard, like body armor, and it smelled disgusting. As a child, I had a coat that also acted as my Kleenex. I too had built up a shiny hard-shell finish on the sleeve, but I was only four and wasn't addicted to mackerel. Though technically still a motorcycle club member, Tommy had been reduced to Hardley Ableson status. Bikers, also known as booger eaters by non-bikers in prison, weren't reaching for the stars when it came to personal hygiene. To make matters worse, Tommy had a fellow booger eater cellmate who was every bit as pungent. They spent most of their time as cell-warrior shut-ins, wafting in the comfort of their seven-by-ten, oblivious to the olfactory nightmare they produced.

Tommy's favorite dinner was the stinkin' ass canned fish that was sold on commissary, He cooked his mackerel in the microwave daily with a hefty squirt of squeeze cheese and a wad of fermented jalapeno peppers for a garnish. It filled the cellblock with a hideous smell.

"Who lost their fuckin' lunch?" someone would call out.

A chorus would reply.

"It's fuckin' Tommy cookin' that stinkin' ass mackerel again."

I took over a vacated cell previously occupied by two other booger eaters who lived the same way. It took some serious elbow grease to dislodge the relief sculptures affixed to the walls.

Inmates policed each other when it came to hygiene. Tommy needed policing in the worst way.

Someone took action and arrested Tommy's coat. No longer could Tommy's coat stand at attention and hold its arms straight out like snot plastic. It was supple.

"Who washed my fucking COOAAAT!" he yelled in a primal scream. He still had a respectable set of lungs as it was heard throughout the housing unit.

A ripple of stifled laughs and snickering filled the cellblock. Some showed a semblance of respect and acknowledged the treasonous act that had taken place with the statement, "that's fucked up," a universal expression of empathy in prison. No one knew who washed his coat, and no one was saying.

We all had our suspicions. I have to believe it was Jimmy the Shoe, from the shit eatin' grin stuck to Jimmy's mug. Jimmy the Shoe earned his name the hard way. He was thrown out of a vehicle onto a freeway when he was twenty. The empty vehicle went on without him. His blood alcohol level probably saved his life. The accident shortened his left femur bone by about three inches. He was also in a coma and wore diapers before having to learn to walk and talk again. He had grown up in the California juvenile system before moving on to the D.O.C and then the feds where I met him. Concrete and gray steel is all he'd ever known: a convict poster child covered in tattoos neck to knuckles. In the middle of his ink storm one could just make out Mister ZigZag, who had started it all and was made from a combination of melted black checker pieces and soot from burnt notebook paper, tattoo ink made with county jail ingenuity. Jimmy was crazy enough to police Tommy's coat, I figured.

Once formidable, Tommy no longer stayed in shape by breaking down greasy motors or cooking methamphetamine. Tommy was now a senior citizen on the decline, white-haired and diminished by time, settling into the last sad chapter of his life. But no one doubted he still had one good stabbing left in him if he was to identify the treasonous cleaning culprit who rinsed away his biker pride.

Jimmy the Shoe never copped to it. Nobody would.

I've never seen a biker cry, but on that day I came close.

Whenever the madness got too much, I'd retreat to the band room and bang on the drums, but sometimes the madness found me even there. When a certain Skinhead was interested in learning the drums and started a death metal band, I was asked to teach a little. I obliged. They practiced hard and got a lot louder. Earplugs were a coveted item. I always kept a pair with me from working in the factory.

"What should we name our band?" Tax asked me.

Seeing as how there were four of them, my natural response was, "How about the foreskins?"

"We thought of that, but it's already been taken," he answered.

They settled on "Phallus Cooper" as a solid second choice. I'm still waiting for their first C.D. to come out.

Chapter 48
The Hustle

Everyone needs a hustle in prison if they want to enjoy any creature comforts and leave prison with some bank. Some guys cleaned cells. Some would do special-order laundry, which could include pressed gear for visits or delivered clothes. Kitchen workers smuggled food. There were sports books and stores. And, of course, drug dealers, vintners, tattoo artists and prostitution to name a few.

Working in the bakery was one of the most coveted and high paying jobs in prison because of the access to yeast. A small amount was enough to kick off a bag of wine. Easily concealed under the scrotum, at least that's what they tell me. Even the most zealous prison guard would usually miss it in his pat-down search. The vintners need the yeast to keep the drinking masses happy and make their "pruno" or prison wine. They would pay a tidy sum to a reliable source.

It seemed like every housing unit had the equivalent of a town drunk. This is a person who has trouble holding down a job, keeping a place to live, continuously gets in fights and trouble with the law, just like they did back in society.

They'd just carry their addiction and their havoc-making right on inside with them. The town drunk often stirred racial tensions until kept in check by one of his own—by whatever method available.

Vintners jumped comical hoops to get their product to market and stay one step ahead of "The Man." Like a scene from *The Untouchables* during prohibition, the guards would conduct constant unit searches. Moving pruno from cell to cell to avoid detection during its gestation period was crucial. Wine merchants made product in the dish room all the time because like a romance novel, it was hot and steamy and it cooked real fast. Trouble was they couldn't get it out of the chow hall, so guys were often drunk on the job just like in the real world. It wasn't the easiest hustle, but the vintners, the yeast-in-the-scrotum mules, and the product storage keepers all cashed in, making apple wine, raisin jack, tomato paste wine and other varieties. The vision of making the leap to hard alcohol was always dreamed of but never realized.

Like the Yeasty Boys, I figured out right away that I'd need to develop a source of extra income. Yes, I'm thankful for the taxpayers that footed the bill for my food and housing, but any extras were on me. Tennis shoes, coffee, cigarettes, zoo zoos and wham whams (prison slang for sweets-n-treats), writing tablets, decent soap that wouldn't strip your skin off, and toothpaste were staples. Shower shoes were a must. You didn't want to be without shower shoes.

My hustle was fudge, Con Fections. I wanted these guys to be in a good mood. I developed quite a reputation with my micro-fudgery. The business skills I honed in my various businesses, like marketing and distribution, pot dealer, and forged concert ticket seller were useful. Turns out I had skills.

I made small batches in the cellblock microwave, careful never to use Tommy's mackeralwave. My mules would ferry the dry ingredients from the bakery to the housing units for their cut of the proceeds. Sometimes they were successful, other times not so much, depending on the friskiness of the guards' pat down. I offered peanut butter fudge, coffee fudge, and fudge with nuts. Coffee coconut was my best seller. I set and made my goal of 15 percent profit. This allowed me plenty of room for ample free samples. Guards turned a blind eye for the most part as they had bigger fish to fry. Slow and steady wins the race. I became an institution within the institution.

Five pounds a week for years, now that's a ton o' fudge.

Now that I'm out, I think from time to time about using the old business skills for good, like say, making bread and going into competition with Dave's Killer Breads. Mine would be called Heels Only for the not-so-well healed, but I'd need to purchase a multitude of very skinny bread making machines. And then what would I do with the non-heels? That would be a concern. Can you say pigeons?

Chapter 49
Catfish

Catfish was a one-time World Kick Boxing Association number two, as in on the planet. You say that Catfish is a bad mutha? Shut yo mouth. After losing the fight for freedom, he started conducting "I will beat the shit out of you" classes in prison disguised as Thai Chi, the art of fighting with yourself. Considered to be potentially the baddest dude inside the fence, people, including the guards, gave him a wide berth. We were all very careful around him in words and in actions… with the exception of one genius named Slaughter who ran his mouth and was welcomed into the Catfish beauty salon for a little touch up on his eyeliner.

Catfish and I shared a love of music. Him, a killer blues harmonica player, and me, a bank robber slash drummer. We got along. I trusted in the power of music. He approached me for an $85 loan to buy some new harmonicas through commissary.

Lending came with a fair amount of risk beyond the potential clash with a stone-cold killer. If a person gets "punked," or overtly taken advantage of in prison, the weasels come out of the woodwork demanding this or that 'til the end of the person's time or until they are forced to put a stop to it through an act of violence. A difficult choice under any circumstances, it's the one most often made to reestablish respect on the yard, but with the added bonus of getting more time in the process. The alternative for them would be to P.C. up. That is, ask to be taken out of the main population and put into The Hole for protective custody. Time in P.C. is the slowest time possible.

All this weighed into my decision. If Catfish stiffed me, an act of violence might be a suicidal choice in addition to all of the above.

After rejecting the council of my peers, I decided to roll the dice. I obliged. We set up a 0-percent A.P.R., six-month payment plan, and unlike me, he never missed a beat. To the surprise of most, he did me right. He may have been a killer, but he hit the right note with me. We played music together for a few more years before my time was up.

Overall, the deeper I went into my sentence, the more I paid attention to the inmates I socialized with, who I talked with, and how I spent my time. The further removed from the cloud of crack smoke I got, the more my thoughts about most everything changed. All around me were people who reminded me of those back in the shooting galleries back home. But there were also surprising people with a lot to offer. A big part of living right was choosing right, starting with the people I associated with.

My quest for intelligent conversation wasn't limited to race, only gender, by default. Come to find out, all the geniuses were locked up. A group of Mensa geniuses would solve mathematical puzzles together for braggin' rights.

Riddle me this Batman, what are you doing here?

I had the utmost respect for many, like a former Thai general. At age sixty, he had the choice of being a free man or thirty years in prison to keep his holdings in Thailand so that his family wouldn't be destitute. He took the time and kept his pride.

Chapter 50

D.A.P.

The judge sent me to the Sheridan, Oregon prison in part for geographical reasons, but also because of the in-house, year long, drug and alcohol treatment program. She had an inkling that I needed some help. That's why she's the judge.

Prison officials offered one year off the sentence of any non-violent offender who completed the cognitive-emotive therapy program. After settling into the prison routine, with still just one oar in the water, I decided I would wait until I got a bit closer to my release date to enroll.

I blew it.

The classification for unarmed bank robbery changed from non-violent to violent. I clamored to get the year off but arrived too late to the party. In dice, this is called crapping out. "No year off for you." I decided to enroll anyway. It may help save me a prison sentence or two down the road, I thought.

This program had brochures about rational Ralph and irrational Rachel. The dysfunctional, not-so-healthy cartoon couple possessed a wealth of useful information for us wayward convicts on how *not* to act if we were ever to become cartoons.

My group consisted of a handful of twisted characters.

Old Dave had been the head of a Minneapolis low-income housing development. While drunk, which was most of the time, he developed a bell curve model projecting revenues that didn't exist. As a result, he received million-dollar tax returns from the I.R.S. from money never earned. After about the third such return, they got a little pissed off.

Velvel, Yiddish for Wolf meaning "mighty, fearless warrior from the tribe of Benjamin," became my cellie. Oh, how Velvel wanted to be a Viking. I suggested a horned yarmulke disguised as a religious head covering to be fabricated in the upholstery section of the furniture factory and sanctioned by the chaplain. Once properly attired, he could submit an additional request to the warden for some rowing machines to bolster Viking authenticity. Can you imagine him thinking my suggestions ridiculous? And so his dream of being the first hybrid Dead Sea Viking accepted into the Wiccan sweat lodge contingency died on the vine. His pillaging and plundering would have to live only in his dreams.

Velvel didn't look like a Wolf or a warrior. He resembled an English sheep dog with glasses. He was a chain smoker without a toothbrush. Bad combo. I know that Hasidic Jews have some washing rituals, but this guy had an aversion to soap and water. I had the top bunk because I was able to hoist my skinny ass up there.

Because he had wolf droppings stuck in his fur, he forced me into action after three nights of enduring the wafting from below. He was as greasy as an 18th-century Swedish farmer who had been sewn into his clothes. I threw all his dirty clothing and detritus out onto the tier while being cheered on by the rail hangers. There was always a crowd waiting for something to happen. I pronounced him homeless until he cleaned up his act. To his credit, he made an effort and no longer had to wander in the wilderness.

Six Nine was an airport drug and money courier. Think Quentin Tarantino's movie Jackie Brown, only taller and not as good-looking. He claimed to have never known what was in the valise, and to his surprise the judge didn't say, "Well then, you can go on home now." Being six-foot-nine he didn't blend in that well at the airport. He was a soft-spoken, gentle guy in our group, which also included Bill. I knew the Navy had mess cooks, but Bill was a Navy meth cook. I hadn't heard of that government program before. A couple more meth cooks, two more bank robbers and a Mexican drug cartel member rounded out our little group.

The ten of us spent a year together.

We made charts and grafts and had endless wrap sessions about how to do things differently than Ralph and Rachel, verbally mending the error of our ways. The staffers in the drug and alcohol program (D.A.P.) weren't guards, but highly skilled professionals who did seem to care about us. The program had a big impact on me, and I'm extremely grateful. People who did not take the program looked upon those who did with suspicion. The so-called *real convicts* viewed it as the R.A.T. program, not the D.A.P. program. With a sentence reduction off the table, few took advantage, unable to think of other benefits: like changing, like not coming back to prison, like recovering from addiction and crime. I can only have compassion knowing that small minds breed contempt. The chances are that those naysayers are still behind bars looking at the good with a wary eye.

That year went by at an accelerated rate, and I did have some fun. Strange as it may seem, prison wasn't all bad though I wouldn't sign up again. My sentence was just the right size, one day less and who knows?

Chapter 51
Dr. No

There was an epidemic of sorts going on. There were an ungodly number of participants in the D.A.P. program developing Bells Palsy, a virus that makes a person look like they had a stroke. The normal ratio is one-in-seventy people will develop Bells Palsy sometime in their life. I counted twelve out of about 110 getting it within a year. I don't know if it was in the water or the staff had contracted with Dr. Swango to keep us in check, but I took it as a sign to keep my shit together.

My experience with Prison doctors is bad. Real bad. The rumor around the yard was that our in-house prison doctor had been caught doling out an overabundance of narcotics to prostitutes and the like. He was then sentenced to work for the Bureau of Prisons. This doctor was big as a house and looked none too healthy. For me, this was a question mark, like jogging while smoking cigarettes. His demeanor was on the nasty end of the spectrum. I don't believe he lost too much sleep over it. I lost plenty of sleep, however, when I broke my leg.

Kemo, the 300-pound king of the Hawaiians, broke my leg during a softball game. He nailed me with the ball while I ran to first base. He didn't break my leg on purpose though he was more than capable. He liked me. And I never mentioned his 300-pound "man-girlfriend." In fact nobody did. Nobody was going to say to him, "Oh, and by the way Kemo, that's a dude, just so you know."

All of that aside, I wasn't too happy about breaking my leg. A trip to see the large prison doctor made it worse. I got it x-rayed then was told to get lost by our genius staff doctor.

I sought a second opinion from a real doctor, the infamous Dr. Jeffrey MacDonald, the Green Beret convicted in 1970 for the gruesome murders of his wife and children. McDonald, who maintains his innocence and who is most likely never getting out, offered me a quick diagnosis.

"Yep, broken," he said.

Seventeen days later after plenty of self-care and a lot of delivered meals from my homeboys, it still hurt like hell. I sought another hearing with the prison doc, who made his second diagnosis, "Yep, broken." It was finally put in a cast.

Then, eight days later I was called, via intercom, back to the infirmary and taken out of my cast. Diagnosis: "We made a mistake. Not broken." I wondered what matchbook company had sold him his diploma. Fortunately, cast or no cast, my femur was on the mend. Eventually, I was back running and lifting weights.

A lot of injuries happen on the weight pile from novice lifters trying to do too much. Hello. I was careful and mindful of my form. This didn't stop me from developing a minor tear in my lower abdomen. Diagnosis this time: "Inguinal hernia." Thankfully, I would have this taken care of at the Willamette Valley Medical Center by a real doctor.

The guards snatched me out of my cell and threw me in The Hole, the prison within the prison, awaiting a van ride to the hospital. The operation was covert, just in case my mother or sister should try to intervene and spring me free. After safely shackled, feet, hands and waist and on the road, I settled in and enjoyed the scenery. We drove right by The Spruce Goose, Howard Hughes' wooden monstrosity and arrived at the hospital. I talked to the doc; he described a very small tear on the other side as well, both of which needed repair. Kevlar mesh, the same material used in bulletproof vests, was to be used on me though I doubt it would stop a bullet down there.

Back at the cellblock, after the painkiller (one pill) wore off and my Texaas grapefruit sized testicles' swelling went down, ("Holy fucking shit that hurts," I said often...), I noticed that one of my twins wasn't exactly swinging. I felt certain something was seriously amiss. Lefty was stuck and hard as a rock; I feared he was not long for this world. I took this dire information back to Dr. I Don't Give A Fuck. Need I say more about his response? I made phone calls to family. I did research in the library. I had the prison chaplain talk to a state senator he knew. I acquired copies of the operation medical reports. My sister Vicki called Washington D.C. and talked to the head doctor for the Bureau of Prison. I'd cut no corner in the preservation of my manhood.

After consulting the medical books in the law library, I diagnosed myself with testicular homicide due to the cutting off of the blood supply as a result of the spermatic cord being sewn into Kevlar mesh. The doctor's diagnosis, testicular atrophy due to "fuck off." Medical wheels turned as slowly as a watched clock. Miraculously, my concerns were ready to be addressed seven weeks later.

Guards once again shackled me up and carted me off back to the hospital for an ultrasound. At this point, I had been away from society for seven years. The very attractive professional looking young female ultrasound tech made it all a surreal experience. While shackled to the hospital bed, she applied the jelly to my recently deceased testicle and went round and round and round and round. It went on and on and on and on. She did a very thorough job. I prayed to God that I wouldn't stand up and be noticed. My prayers were answered. Damnit.

After my return to Man Land, I told my story and became the envy of the joint. I was practically givin' out autographs. Many convicts would have been willing to give their left nut for such an experience. After another five weeks, I was once again shackled up and carted off. They went back in and removed a portion of my manhood and offered me a prosthetic. I wondered what my choices were. I considered a Faberge crystal egg. The Hope Diamond for some needed bling seemed fashionable. Instead, I stoically declined and went through a long period of mourning. I wondered how many others had suffered the same fate and envisioned secret rooms in the hospital filled with jars of testicles floating in formaldehyde. Dark days, indeed. I was considering becoming a Brigittine Monk. I had the fudge making down, I'm bald, and I certainly didn't think I'd need my lone cajone. All that was missing was a robe and some faith.

Back at the cellblock, after the wake, my second recovery period began.

"Dude, you're rich" was the consensus.

I began daydreaming about how I would spend my millions. Everyone was certain my lost testicle lawsuit would turn into the goose that laid me a golden egg. I decided this in conjunction with my future city councilman's salary would make a comfortable living. Upon release, the golden egg shrank like my missing testicle. It went from millions to thousands down to zero. Seems no one would touch it. Like "good dude" convicts, doctors don't rat on doctors and lawyers don't represent ex-convicts. I've managed to survive adequately without the millions, thank you very much. My needs have all been met. With my grief behind me, it turns out I don't need two. I'm doing just fine with just one, according to my wife.

A couple years later, after I was released back into the wild world of modern medicine, I started experiencing pain in Ace, my sole survivor. I saw yet another doctor, Dr. Risk. After examining me, he sent one of his minions to give his recommendation.

"It's going to have to come out."

A freakout ensued.

Since I had no intentions of joining the Mormon Tabernacle Choir, I solicited yet another second opinion regarding my diminishing components. I went to a vascular specialist and told her the other doctor's recommendation.

"Ha! Ha! Ha! Ha! Ha!" she said in a machine-gun staccato. "That's crazy, you've got some swelling. Take some ibuprofen, and wear a jock strap."

I took half of her advice, and the problem was solved.

I thought Dr. Risk would fit right in working at the prison.

Chapter 52
Campers

Quite a compound we had in the Willamette Valley, where the fog rolled in and the occasional *detrimental to your health* type situation went down. We were surrounded by two razor wire fences that stood high up on a bank with a ten-foot, no-man's-land in between. Guards would do a continual patrol of the perimeter with shotguns in their pickup trucks just in case an opportunity for target practice on an inmate presented itself.

But oh, how different it was in the comparative paradise that existed on the other side of the fence in the minimum-security camp. You could hear the campers over there having fun all day long, a real party. I wasn't jealous. I never really liked camping anyway. For some, this would be what's considered a "trick bag," a no-win situation. An inmate's security level would drop after he's comfortably settled into a routine with a job at the factory or income from some other hustle. Then it would all be turned upside down. He'd be told to "roll 'em up." Translation, pack your bags.

The transition to a prison with no fence was too much for some to bear. Seeing as how everyone called each other

Dog, ("What's up dog, why you gotta do me like that Dog? Yo Dog" Believe that, Dog") there should have at least been an invisible fence.

Lake Crabtree, named after the Warden, was supposed to be a deterrent. More like a swamp than a lake, it proved a minor obstacle at best. But for Stump, the walk was too much. He set out on his escape across Lake Crabtree using his prosthetic leg as a combination paddle/flotation device. Though short on time left to serve, and short on brains, the need to win back love lost sent him exploring Lake Crabtree and ill-gotten freedom. Once across, he needn't have worried about walking. Staff made sure a ride was waiting for him, though not to Lovers Lane but back to the real prison to listen to the campers have fun.

Back on my side of the razor wire, the powers that be upped the security level from medium to medium-high. Violent prisoners who hadn't been in trouble for a while transferred from high-security prisons. This forced many in my prison to go "camping" with ten years or more left on their sentence and to be trusted to not just walk away.

Many folded up like a K-mart lawn chair and were back with time to spare. More time on their sentence and back in the comfort of the real prison, home sweet home. I met a lot of guys along the way who would sabotage their release because it's the only life they've ever known. They were more afraid of being out than being in.

Shortly before my release I contracted Short Timers Disease. I had witnessed the suffering from this before. Now, it was my turn. I would freak out. I could not concentrate or even communicate. I was filled with anxiety about what was in store for me. I think it turned out O.K.

The fantasy of escape lived inside everyone, if not for themselves, definitely for one of the lifers. There were no pin-up girls hiding the tunnels to freedom that were dug with a spoon. Besides, we ate with plastic sporks. Cells were constantly tossed for the purpose of gleaning information about possible escape attempts and contraband. Some searches were respectful, leaving behind everything in order. Some guards were less kind in other searches and thrashed the contents as much as possible.

My band mate little Johnny had thirty-one years and had been down about eight when he was rounded up and shipped off. He confided in another band mate who had been released about a year earlier. After racking up another serious charge post release, the rat band mate in turn confided to the authorities about Johnny's planned escape to save his ass. Multiple passports with Johnny's photo on them were confiscated from a house, and we never saw him again.

Cell Warriors tried to escape via sleep. They never left their cells through the miracle of pill line. Not an ideal cellie. I escaped through living my life to the fullest and being active day in and day out. The effect was that the calendar pages seemed to turn at a rapid rate.

Chapter 53
Lompoc Loco

Man, could Howly Frank play the guitar. He would bring tears to my eyes. He was a white Hawaiian, very tough, a solid convict who minded his own business. I was runnin' point, (being a lookout), while he got a tattoo on his lower back, a notoriously painful area to get inked. That shit must have hurt because in a very low voice he was screaming his ass off.

"Aaaaaaaahhhhh," he would whisper through clenched teeth, "how much longer 'til we're done? Aaaaaaahhhhhhhh. So uh what do you think, ten more minutes? Aaaaaaahhhhh."

Frank got celled up with Danny, who was one of the Lompoc Penitentiary crazies that had arrived on the scene. Lompoc was a maximum-security, maximum-violence prison that was bursting at the seams. The powers that be figured shipping its problems to other prisons already stuffed far beyond capacity would fix everything. Danny had already been down 20-plus years, and his security level dropped to medium-high. He had been on his best behavior for the previous twelve years after he stabbed his cellie over a perceived slight. The powers that be considered him new-

and-improved and now he was with us at Sheridan, which was also at twice its intended population. He had no gang affiliation. But he tried hard to act "too hard for the yard." He was ready to pick what he considered low-hanging fruit. How he stayed alive all those years is a mystery. He was skinny as a rail, a driven dope fiend with bad manners and worse intentions.

Prison Golden Rule number one: don't be snoopin' in your cellie's shit. Not even in the toilet. And especially not in any way connected to a guy's family. Danny didn't live by any rules, especially golden ones.

Howly Frank loved his Mom and called her regularly. Turns out so did Danny. Danny had somehow become obsessed and acquired Frank's mother's telephone number. He called her collect and attempted to extort money from her. "If you don't pay me, I'll hurt your baby boy," that kind of a thing.

When Danny's gig was up, we knew what he had due him. I had a vested interest and wanted Howly Frank to stay on the yard. He was my friend, and I played music with him on occasion. Regardless, this had to be done.

Frank suited up with steel toe boots and leather gloves. The fact that Danny was a killer wasn't a deterrent for Frank. After late night count and lockdown, they were safely snuggled into their cell. Howly Frank caught a bout of restless leg syndrome as he proceeded to kick the shit out of Danny. Being of Irish descent, Frank made use of the undetectable River Dance technique. The guards were eventually alerted to Danny's unfortunate demise. They took their time. A documented notorious scumbag, even the guards hated him. Danny was off to the hospital and Frank to The Hole. Due to the circumstances, prison officials considered justice served. Frank re-emerged thirty days later. Danny was never seen by any of us again. He probably ended up at an East Coast prison with a scheme to call someone else's mother, whispering threats through his wired shut jaw.

You meet way too many people inside, like Danny, that you can tell are bad news.

Others, not so much.

Dr. Death was comfortable with his new surroundings. The inmate population knew nothing about this guy yet. The staff knew. His situation was *hush hush* by prison officials. Sheridan was just supposed to be a stopover while the Feds got a big indictment together. I was always on the lookout for intelligent conversation. We were both runners, and I ran the track with him a few times making small talk wondering if he was a solid inmate.

My answer was just around the corner.

Seems his reason for living centered on how to poison people.

"And then you add the strychnine and watch their eyes explode, mmmhhhwwaaaaaa," he'd say.

I'd been around a lot of killers and felt no threat, but I had to wonder if the body count would have increased if this guy had been allowed to hang around awhile.

Dr. Death was watching a show in the T.V. room with a score of other inmates. True Crime Dateline N.B.C. or its equivalent, the kind that played the same clips over and over again. His mug shot appeared over and over again on the screen and burnt the image into our minds. The viewing audience was told that he was a physician who had intentionally killed upwards of sixty people via poison, either orally or intravenously. He roamed the earth, kicked out of one country after another, leaving a trail of bodies behind. Heads spun around from the doc to the screen and back again. Cool as a cucumber, he got up and strolled to the guard's office and checked himself into protective custody over concern for his life. A credentialed serial killer had been in our midst. He'll live out his days underground in the United States Prison at Florence, Colorado, a super-max with the worst of the worst and never see the light of day.

Chapter 54
The Birds

One of the more pleasant things about the prison yard was the flocks of birds that shared it with us. I liked the birds. They certainly weren't big enough to carry me away, so I didn't think they were a flight risk. But, I guess some thought they were more of a nuisance, like the warden, for example. As it turned out, the warden held the only opinion that mattered. He ordered hundreds of birds euthanized. There were dead birds everywhere and the inmates who cleaned the grounds filled up hefty bags. Seeing all that avian carnage heightened my sense of paranoia.

Who would fill the bags if we were next?

A pervasive rumor circulating throughout the federal prison system was that if there were a national emergency on a grand scale, we would get locked in our cells and F.E.M.A. would come in and gas us. Then 9/11 hit, and we were all on lockdown. Any inmate who had an issue with the government was rounded up and taken away. Some came back, and others disappeared. The rumor seemed possible to me and more than disconcerting.

I had developed the habit of listening to Art Bell on the late-night fringe radio. According to Art, Y2K was going to wreak havoc, and there'd be hell to pay if we didn't get ready. Many of us whipped each other into a frenzy while debating the ramifications. I believed that because I was locked up I was a goner. The warden would pump us as full of gas as he did all those annoying birds. But my sister Vicki could still be saved, which became my anxiety-filled mission in what I was sure was the short time I had left on this Earth. I tried talking her into quitting her civil service job of twenty-plus years so she could head for the hills. She would need canned goods, a lot of water and one of those $59.95 hand-crank radios that Art Bell advertised on his show. With that radio, she could commiserate with the all the other unemployed postal workers who had thrown it all away to survive. Hope she doesn't run into Sasquatch out there!

"Doug, I'm really not prepared to retire right now," Vicki said.

It turned out to be a very practical response. I definitely drank the Kool-aid.

When you live in an alternate universe for an extended period, it's hard to know what's reality and what's not. My reality inside seemed as foreign to me as my family's reality of life outside. Only in visiting rooms did those two lives intersect.

The last time I saw my father was when he visited me in the joint in 1997. He had driven my mother down from Seattle even though they hated each other. Our time was spent with Ill Will verbally assaulting my mother and attempting to make her feel small, which had been his M.O. all of my life. I went back to the cell-block and issued my own no-contact order. I vowed never to see him again.

The visiting room was a place where visions for a better tomorrow were discussed, stories told, and packages of dope swallowed. The visitor would hide the small package under their tongue and spit it into the mouth of the inmate mule to continue traveling its dangerous journey through their digestive tracks. If the package ruptured, the odds of an accidental overdose and death increased dramatically. If successful in transit, the package would be readied for market. This involved the smuggler digging through their excrement and preparing the package while hoping the product had not gotten tainted. It is considered poor customer service if the product kills its user when injected into the bloodstream. The process was less than foolproof.

One would think this high failure rate would be a deterrent. One would be wrong. The 1-to-100 street-to-prison value was too tempting for those with big balls and small brains. In prison, that describes a lot of us. As a result, the visiting room was like the Tijuana border crossing.

Everyone is on camera in the visiting room. Those suspected of smuggling drugs were dry celled, meaning no running water, as in no toilet. An inmate, a plain concrete box and a bucket. This also meant no clothing. The only thing wet in that cell were cans of prune juice, as many as you wanted. Like the United States Postal Service, whether rain or shine, sleet or snow, they never failed to deliver the package on time. Try as a mule might to fight it, the cheek squeezers would never disappoint. Kind of hard to come up with a backup plan at that point. I can't imagine a lot of guards raised their hands for that assignment. Upon release back to main population, the paperwork was processed to add another five years to that man's sentence.

As an added measure to fight the war on drugs, the powers that be decided to purchase what I'll call the Electro Bad Ass Bad Guy Super Surveillance Wand. This slick gizmo would detect even the minutest of drug contraband. It reminded me of me, in my pre-prison using days, when I fought my war on drugs: I took them off the streets one gram at a time, intravenously.

Vicki got to see the Electro Bad Ass Bad Guy Super Surveillance Wand in action. She was a smart consumer. She bought sustainable, fashionable clothing in the latest styles and colors that happened also to set off all the sirens and buzzers that alerted the prison staff of an imminent threat. After she had endured the helpful hands of the prison guards in a pat-down search, the Sherlock Holmes guards figured out my sister's shirt was the culprit. Hemp, that all-purpose durable fabric, tried and true. It was Reefer Madness all over again. She was taken away and made to discard her newly purchased shirt. Somehow a new article of clothing was to materialize. One of the sober volunteers, who hosted meetings in the prison, volunteered the needed garb to Vicki. The prison survived the serious threat of my sister's hemp clothing.

It's hard to put into words the panic and helplessness I felt in prison when I learned Vicki was M.I.A. She had been rock steady my whole life. She was there for me at sentencing and visited twice a year like clockwork. She took care of our brother Bill when he was dying from A.I.D.S. and watched as he lost his mind. She was super-human. I looked at her with admiration and awe.

I was sober enough that I had started to feel my feelings again. Vicki's disappearance and my worry turned me into a bit of a mess. When she did resurface she asked me for guidance. I realized I couldn't be a mess and help her. But, I couldn't grasp how I could be of any help from behind the prison walls. It was selfish of me. I hadn't realized that other people, besides me, would have demons to exercise. Then I remembered the phrase,

"No matter how far down the scales we have gone we can see how our experience can benefit others."

I saw a lot of guys try like hell to manage their family's lives via the pre-pay telephone to no avail. I couldn't do that. But I could give my sister some benefit of what I had learned.

"Give up," I told her. "That's what I did."

I was afraid I would lose the most important person in my life. In my using days, I had no clue just how insidious drugs were until it was too late. I prayed that Vicki would come back, and she did.

Chapter 55
Self-Prescribed Tom

The defunding of mental health facilities in our country created a glut of low-level offenders occupying space in the prison system when they should have been receiving treatment. A lot of these guys felt backed into a corner. They'd lash out at other inmates, thus becoming high-level offenders and ending up at Sheridan F.C.I.

Inmates are MacGyver clones. They can make anything out of anything. They can use discarded items for myriad applications. Never is the cliché "one man's trash is another man's treasure," truer. These mentally ill people, society's trash, were soon used for other purposes than intended: inmate's treasure.

When a serious junkie ran out of options for smuggled narcotics, often Plan B was put in play: appropriate psych meds from Mr. Pill Line. Mr. Junkie would persuade Mr. Pill Line, who is unemployable even in prison, to give up their meds for a small fee, usually cigarettes or coffee. A bevy of problems ensued: The unknown effects on the new user, the known effects on the prescribed user and the effects on anyone in their wake.

Tom, a schizophrenic, took a combination of two drugs, one used to address what was going on in his head and one for his body. One does not work without the other. When his body froze, he had his arm extended, finger pointing, with his mouth and eyes wide open. He looked like he was alerting everyone to an upcoming disaster. We waited and waited and yet, there was no disaster except for Tom, who was stuck like that for four hours.

Plotting and scheming to beat others out of their meds was a year-round sport, often with threats of violence. Tom was one of the lucky ones, he got to make choices because he got looked after by a certain someone known to take serious action against anyone who fucked with Tom.

Tom was by no means the only odd duck. One lived with me named Canvasback. With a ring name like Canvasback, you'd have thought he never won a fight. On the contrary, Frankie was 17-0 as a professional boxer. But Frankie liked to gamble and needed a big score. He was known by the feds to be friendly with local organized crime. With this information and the threat of prison time, the Conspiracy Wranglers (DEA) approached Frankie with a deal.

The gist of their proposition was "We'll give you a boat load of money, you buy the necessary equipment and ingredients, start making meth so we can bust those we know to be already involved in the distribution network. How's that sound?"

Frankie's response was "Sure, I'll take your money."

With his new found fortune he disappeared into the gamblers lair—he had a weakness for the ponies—only to turn up broke at a later date. Hilarious to some, the DEA was not laughing and indicted him on Conspiracy to Manufacture Methamphetamine even though he never intended to do anything of the sort. He was sentenced to thirty-one years with seventeen years of supervised release. At age fifty, this was a death sentence.

No one I knew believed Frankie capable of making even a cup of coffee, let alone following a complicated recipe to make meth.

He was my cellmate for two years and taught me how to box by punching me in the chest and arms every day at four o'clock stand-up count. That was how he showed me tough love. He was fond of me. In Frankie's case, once a boxer, always a boxer. I learned to fight back.

His constant shtick was shadow boxing with a cigarette hanging out of his mouth. To any normal person, Canvasback just looked insane. With no one normal in sight, this was just another part of our daily scenery. He would look at someone menacingly delivering a flurry of hooks and jabs into the air and then look around to see if someone else wanted some of that.

Being a truly afflicted gambler, currency or not, he offered several humiliating stunts instead of payment to other gamblers. One pack of cigarettes equaled a Wormy Dog. After losing his bet, Frankie would be on display to an audience of about three hundred in the chow hall scooting his butt across the floor and barking like a dog. Being a good sport, he never welched on one of those bets. He was totally O.K. with his version of downward dog.

Piotter 250

Chapter 56
Made in America

Prison industries are a multi-billion dollar endeavor. At Sheridan F.C.I. we made furniture: credenzas, tables for judge's chambers, office chairs and bureaus to name a few. Other prisons in the fed system made mattresses, lockers, clothing, protective gear, boots, toothbrushes and on and on. Prisoners made everything that we used on a daily basis. In theory, the furniture was sold to government agencies only, but I remember a flap about some boxer shorts ending up at Sears. The feds even have an online office supply furniture store, so prisoners made a lot of things normal people used on a daily basis, too. Like inmates, the prison system has its hustle.

There are 217,000 people in the federal prison system in the U.S. There were 1,200 in my prison, of which 300 worked in the factory. That's a whole lot of workers nationwide making a lot of stuff. Made in the U.S.A., who says the manufacturing sector is dead?

I worked in the hardwood mill preparing the wood through a seemingly endless string of machinery, like planers, gang line rip saws, double-end miters, vertical-bore drills, shapers, sand masters and on and on. Accidents happen, usually because Mr. Macho Know It All believed he knew how to run that machine because he "ain't no pussy." When feeding a board through the thirty-inch planer, it's important to have enough length so your fingers are away from the table. It's also important to start feeding it in at an angle so the blades don't grab it all at once making it jump. Mr. Bad Ass Skinhead attempted to send a twelve-inch long board straight through with his fingers underneath for support. The board kicked up and slammed back down pulverizing his middle finger.

They had a pin put into his finger with the bone shards wrapped around it for the attempted save. Having to elevate it so it would be above his heart and not throb, he appeared to be giving us all the finger, likely the last time he'd shoot the bird to anyone with that hand. I saw it coming, but it was not my place to say anything. In prison, you mind your business.

Even at work, there wasn't always a lot going on other than cards, book reading or working on a special project. So when a tour of judges or investors headed up by our fearless leader, The Warden, came through the factory, our mill bosses told us to "look busy." Every machine would get turned on at once, oak and ash planks fed through the planer, carts of this or that moved around, a beehive of activity for three minutes. When they left, we were quiet as church mice.

At work, my war with a guy named Cliff started over territory. We both worked on the shaper, me during the day and he, swing shift. I don't recall who started it, but it involved our boots. There were free boots, and there were good boots. And the good boots were hard to come by. The laundry workers had access to all the clothing because it was all stored there, and they got paid for their hustle. I paid to get good boots. When leaving my shift at the factory, I changed into tennis shoes because my steel-toed boots would set off the metal detectors creating a log jam of pissed off inmates if I had to stop and take them off.

The next day shift, my laces were gone. The next swing shift, one of Cliff's tongues was missing. Then, the next day shift there was holes drilled in my boots with dowels sticking out. Next, swing shift casters had been screwed onto Cliff's boots. Day shift full of glue. Swing shift heels cut off and screwed to the table.

I've heard of murders over less, but Cliff and I called a truce and ended up getting along. Both our boots were the better for it.

With access to so many cool machines, work orders to fill or not, I stayed busy. I worked with an older guy named Lyle, who was one tough nut. He was under the parole system, which means he would see the parole board and either be deemed fit, or not fit for release. On a fifteen-year sentence, the board may release you in ten and make you successfully comply for five years in supervised release. If a condition wasn't met, that person gets sent back to prison start the five years over again, but remains eligible to see the board in two years and possibly once again let out with five years supervision. Sound confusing? It is. It creates a yo-yo effect that can go on indefinitely, as was the case for Lyle. He did an enormous amount of time far exceeding his original sentence if you added it all up. He could not stay sober.

Lyle had been a musician, logger, mechanic, fisherman, boxer, carpenter, as well as a bank robber and a drunk. He played guitar before losing his thumb to a flywheel and started making guitars instead. Lyle was a genius woodworker. In the factory, he would make wooden steam engines with pistons, wheels and a lot of moving parts. He would graphite the insides of the cylinders then hook it up to the air hose and watch all the moving parts go.

I gleaned as much information as possible working with Lyle and started making wooden motorcycles. Rudimentary at first, they just kept getting better and better. They took about three months to make as I could only work on them sporadically. More than one guard confiscated and kept them, possibly for a gift. The dust collector for the table saw was a favorite stash spot. I never lost one in there. I'm still making motorcycles in my garage at home.

The tool room was essentially a locked cage with a metal Dutch door.

The workers would sit behind the door and pass out the appropriate tools to the specified inmates. They would place a chit indicating which inmate had which tool. If a tool went missing after the tool count at the end of a shift, no one was going anywhere until it was found. If it wasn't found, the person responsible for that tool would go to The Hole, the unemployment line, and a two-year wait to get back into the factory. It was a courtesy to look out for the tools of those you worked with and vice versa. If an inmate had a beef with another, it was not uncommon for a tool to disappear out of spite or jealousy. If someone thought they would move into a coveted job after a certain inmate was gone, they would hide a tool hoping it wouldn't be found. That was a constant. Think about what you could do with a screwdriver in prison.

Chapter 57
Count

Every housing unit had a bookrack. The books in my unit were as old and stale as the hills. The titles were geared for eighth-grade reading levels, which suited me just fine for a time. As a drinker and druggie, I was not much of a reader. When sober I couldn't get enough. Pouring over Louis L'Amour, The Sacketts or the Dick Francis horseshit books eventually didn't cut the mustard. I needed Pat Conroy or Joseph Kanon Cold War spy novels. My sister Vicki came to my rescue. Bless her heart, she sent me about four books a month for years. I soon became the prison librarian. My rule was you read it and pass it on, no selling. There were generally twenty or so on a waiting list as a good book was hard to come by, especially during count.

Anytime I got locked in my cell for any reason, there was a little bit of anxiety associated with it. Four o'clock stand-up count was no different, even though it happened every day. You could pretty much tell if it was going to be a long, drawn-out fiasco by the guards who were working the A & B sides of the unit. They would look in every cell, make a mark in their little notebook and try and come up with the same number. They would radio their numbers to control to make sure all units were correctly counted. Then we waited anywhere from ten minutes to an hour and a half. This would push the clock forward cutting into our dinner time and evening exercise or anything else that was scheduled. Tensions flared.

All units would have to be in sync or a recount occurred. Sync was rare. I would sometimes see them scratching their heads looking at their little notebooks. Then, they would yell "Recount."

It was good to have a book to take your mind off the inanity.

We were counted five times a day, 365 days year. 10 a.m., 4 p.m., 9 p.m. and two in the middle of the night accompanied by the flashlight in the eyes or the kicking of the door. They had to see your face to make sure you didn't pull a Houdini and somehow escape through the keyhole after you were locked in at 11 p.m. Escape was always thought about, especially in the fog bowl. Even talking about escape would cause an inmate to disappear, swept off to a different prison or The Hole for some vague discipline. Staff took it seriously, and there was always an extra set of ears. Though no one at Sheridan succeeded, one guy named Bill, who worked in Construction and Maintenance Services, gave a valiant effort.

Bill was an intense quiet guy who'd been around a long time. He had been an Army Ranger before he was sent in for who knows what and settled into his job in Construction and Maintenance Services. CMS was the most mobile and unsupervised job an inmate could have. They wheeled around carts full of tools from unit to unit fixing things.

Their mobility allowed them to ferry contraband from one place to another. Guards could even see the stuff moving at times, but they didn't always know the value or use of a particular item. It meant getting busted was pretty rare. Bill used his post and his tools to plan his escape.

Fog engulfed us quite often in the fall. It also got windy in the Willamette Valley, a perfect storm for hang gliding if you're willing to take the risk of getting blown into the razor wire. The glider Bill was said to have built had been quite functional and would have probably worked had he made it onto the roof. Somehow, he never got approved for takeoff and was never seen again. We had only snippets of information gleaned from the guards. Nevertheless, Bill became a folk hero.

Chapter 58
Perry

We were without a prison Chaplain for a time during which my small group did not have a structured meeting place to talk recovery. We had to hold clandestine meetings on the yard, which were usually broken up for fear of a plot to overthrow the government. Holding hands for all to see wasn't helping our comfort level either. I complained about this to The Warden.

"If you're having a problem, go see the psychiatrist, and we'll get you on pill line," he told me.

"No disrespect intended sir, but the idea is to get off pills," I pointed out.

Enter Father Perry, a Catholic priest of about sixty-five and a friend to recovering addicts. He was about five-foot-two and 125 pounds, but to me he was huge. He moved like an Everglades Flat Bottom Hydrofoil, with his feet not visible and apparently never touching the ground. Always on the go, he floated this way or that and moved real fast. Perry flew seeds into Bosnia for farmers during the war on his own dime. This was not popular with or sanctioned by the Vatican, who discouraged the adventure. He did it anyway.

The Vatican was not pleased. They needed someone to punish and chose to reprimand him for this horrible act. Perry was transferred from Europe and sentenced to work in the prison.

He told me he was in a period of transition and not long for the robe. He considered retirement and a secular life. He didn't believe that his talents were being utilized by the church hierarchy. An odd Catholic duck, he had been called to serve after being sober almost twenty years. My group, who I refer to as Twelve Angry Men, was a group of twelve out of 1,200 (the one percent) who were trying to stay sober. Perry became our best advocate, and we loved him.

He miraculously changed the mind of the warden and soon we had a place to meet, which brought more men into our group. Perry went to bat for me during my medical mishap, putting himself out there on the behalf of me and my testicle. I talked to him for hours about personal issues. He listened, we prayed, and it was as simple as that.

We could talk about anything, which in prison is very rare.

"How do you deal with the no-sex rule you guys have to follow?" I once asked Perry.

"It's got to come one way or another, be it good or evil," he said. "God gave me two good hands, so every once in a while I'll use one to toss one off. Plus, I came late to the party and indulged plenty when I was young," he said with a laugh.

I thought a masturbating Catholic priest with a sordid past was very impressive.

I spent three, one-hour sessions with him in confession and told him things I've told no one else. I have never been involved with organized religion, but he was qualified and had something to offer, earning my utmost respect in the process.

Speaking of respect, it's hard not to respect the making of a prison tattoo gun, which is likely to be found hidden away in most every prison in America. The fashioning of a prison tattoo gun is pretty ingenious. Here's what's needed: Toothbrush, batteries, motor appropriated from law library cassette player or other machine, ball point pen appropriated from staff member, portion of an E-string from a guitar from the band room, a button, some matches, some tape and some balls.

Take your toothbrush, melt and bend it at the crook where the head meets the handle. Melt the bristles and push them up out of the way. Tape the round motor and 8mm disc, which has a post that spins in the middle to the top of the toothbrush head with the post sticking out 90-degrees to the handle. The batteries get taped to the top of the handle. A conductor will be needed to make the connection, usually aluminum foil. Melt the button onto the motor post so it oscillates. Then tape the barrel of the pen parallel onto the toothbrush handle. Cut a tiny hole in the tip of the pen's ink dispenser allowing the E-string to slide up and down. The E-string is then bent at the top and melted into a buttonhole. The connection is made and the whirring sound of a functional tattoo gun can be heard from nearby cells.

Prison tattoo artists are not short of styles to choose from, some of which are spider webs on the elbows or the face. This can mean a murder of another inmate or just prison time accumulated. Teardrops at the corner of the eyes mean the same thing. Bible verses from the base of the neck to the small of the back mean whatever the Bible verse says, I guess, like a giant Virgin Mary or other religious themes.

The bikers would walk around the outdoor track in a pack, proudly displaying the Harley Davidson tattoos on their backs, revving up their imaginary V-twin motors while making that sound with their lips and tongue. I never saw a biker with a Honda tattoo, but I've never been to a Japanese prison either.

Not all tattoo artists are created equal. Somebody has to be the first customer though usually for free or at a discounted rate. Starting out, the tattoo artist often works on themselves for a time, usually on their forearm or their thighs because it's the easiest part of their body to access. It's like the great barber with the bad haircut, except the practice is permanent.

Mennen Speed Stick was a coveted item for tat artists. It was no longer sold on commissary, but still available on the low down. It was not coveted for its use as a deodorant but to transfer patterns from graphite paper to the body. The real artists could freehand and didn't need patterns. The novice, on the other hand, could use the Speed Stick method, the equivalent of paint by numbers.

The Skinheads had their personal artist who would only work on other Skinheads or those being initiated. Skinheads offer fewer choices. The new member is made to get the anti-Semitic graphic tattoo, often in a highly visible place, like their skull or neck. One I remember as popular in this artist's repertoire was Hitler with his German shepherd stepping on the neck of a Jew wearing a yarmulke. Tough to get a job post-prison with that one, I suspect. I know discrimination is illegal for employers, but if I were covered head-to-toe I wouldn't be helping myself in the already difficult job market.

For some, getting tattoos became an addiction. They couldn't stop. When they ran out of real estate, they would have to start on someone else's body. Nothing was exempt: neck, face, top of the head and all the way down the arms and fingers. It wasn't aesthetically appealing to me. I do have a few tattoos though: a New Orleans jazz scene on my back, a tiny drum set on my right arm, a memorial to my brother Bill on my arm and The Space Needle so I could represent my city. I do regret The Space Needle. The artist was off his game that day. It looks more like the mushroom needle. My jazz scene was done by the best, Pat, a Gypsy Joker biker who shortly after release died of a heroin overdose.

Piotter 264

Chapter 59
Swapping Uniforms

I'm grateful for the availability of the building and trades vocational school that I took while locked up. We built miniature balsa wood houses to scale. Blueprint reading and building codes were just a few of the pertinent subject matters covered that I would employ in my post-prison life. I learned to work hard for my income rather than chase the allure of "big money" that never arrived. I also learned that prison employees were not exempt from the lure of big money either. The temptation often made them something other than rich, something more like bait. Inmates would target a particular staff member who they thought they could groom to serve in their illegal enterprise. Once the hook was in and the staffer had everything to lose, it was on.

Mitch, an instructor who taught me many of the skills I use in my contracting business today felt the hook set soon enough. Mitch had a trusted inmate assistant who helped him and helped us. He was great. Unfortunately, he enforced a role reversal, and the assistant became the instructor—not in building codes—in the art of heroin smuggling.

The groom was a veteran manipulator who knew how to reel one in. He had built a seventy-five-foot-long concrete box underground in the mountains of Idaho and manufactured tons of weed. He netted millions of dollars and twenty years. Mitch was impressed, and together they wanted to recreate the wealth and power that came from that. Neither could see beyond the end of their wallets. The Groom had his people on the streets deliver the package to Mitch, who in turn acted as mule right on into the prison. Once successfully in, Mitch would give it to the Groom for distribution. I once walked in on the groom cutting up some dope right out in the open classroom. He had a fantasy that he was Claude Raines, *The Invisible Man* and apparently pretty comfy with the understanding that he and Mitch had worked out.

Because there are no secrets in prison, Mitch got a turd laid in his punch bowl. I don't know how many times he got away with it, but on this day the gig was up. He was caught smuggling eighty-seven grams of heroin into the institution. The street value was about $4,300. Prison yard value: about half a million. They paraded him around with his head hung low while he wore his own set of handcuffs. I'm sure he disliked the khaki uniforms as much as me. But he would certainly have time to get used to them. As for the Groom, he had to call the whole thing off.

Chapter 60
Ready to Roll

Just prior to being released, the sober volunteers from the streets who came into run our recovery meetings hammered home the idea that I should not make my past life a secret.

"Tell 'em where you've been, who you are and what you've done," they said.

Their council proved to be invaluable. To my astonishment, people wanted to know me. This was new information. I'm now able to blend into a crowd or address one if necessary. From where I came, this is a miracle.

The experience of my past and my sobriety are my most valuable assets. My fellow sober prison travelers and I had a corny phrase we would say to each other: "Can I biggie size that for ya?" This meant we were willing to do whatever it took, even taking a McJob if necessary, to stay out of prison. I did apply for a few McJobs upon my release, but to no avail. The willingness was there, which had never been the case before. It was just one small example of the significant difference from the person that I had been when I got to prison and who I became by the time I got out. When I walked out, I was ready to be the real me, the person that had been missing all along.

Book Four
Welcomed Back

Chapter 61
A Short Leash

The day I was released—October 25, 2001—I waited in the lobby of the prison for my sister Vicki to pick me up. The front door stood wide open. Horvath, a well-respected, kind and decent prison guard said, "You don't have to wait in here. You're free to go. You can wait outside." I raised my eyebrows, poked my head out the door and my body soon followed.

What a strange feeling it was not to have to wait to be told what to do.

On the road, we stopped at an outlet mall.

"Can I buy some shoes?" I asked Vicki.

"You've got money; you don't have to ask me," she said.

I thought, *Man, I could get used to this*.

After a fine first day, Vicki dropped me at the supervised halfway house I had been assigned to live in for the next six months. My first unsupervised excursion beyond the invisible fence is forever etched in my mind. I went to a downtown Seattle drug store to purchase a Wahl trimmer so that I could cut my own hair. As a twenty-year veteran of male pattern baldness, I decided I wasn't pretending anymore. I preferred to take it all the way down to the bone.

As I sat on the bus in my unfamiliar surroundings, I took notice of all the people sitting nearby. Many seemed to be talking to themselves as if we were all on our way together to the nut house. *What the fuck?* I thought.

I had never seen a cell phone before, and this was my introduction. Eventually, I sorted it all out.

I hopped off the Metro bus and looked up into the gloomy post 9/11 October sky where military jets—now part of the "normal" landscape—protected the homeland from would be terrorists. As I stood on the street corner, I found myself in the middle of a sting operation. With guns drawn, two Seattle police officers flew past me and apprehended a suspect who had been on the same bus.

They yelled the usual: "Freeze. Put your hands up."

So I did. It was hardwired. The cops didn't take notice of me as they grabbed their suspect. They body-slammed him and bounced him off the sidewalk right next to me. In the blink of an eye, they cuffed and stuffed him and whisked him away as the crowd, and I looked on. I hadn't moved. I stood still and reached for the heavens. I remembered when I got body-slammed by the police a dozen years earlier in Yakima over some stolen meat.

"Everything's under control folks," I said.

I felt a need to elaborate while I tentatively let down my arms. "It wasn't me."

Despite the odd looks I got, I felt pretty good that for once in my life it wasn't.

Back at the halfway house, things returned to normal and not in the good way. Normal for me was the last decade plus spent in two different prisons and the previous entirety of my existence in flying through Crazyville with an ever-evolving drug of choice. My challenge was to find my new normal. The halfway house was not that. I lived with a guy I knew from prison named Norman, who was what I would call, "touched." He must have been born on the seventh day when God was on a much-needed vacation and his replacement had cut some corners. Norman had deep, dark, eye sockets with a perpetual thousand-yard stare. His mouth gaped open. His bottom lip curled down as if lacking enough energy to stay rooted in place. Smacking his melon against the cell's cement block wall was one of his favorite pastimes. This, I believe, stemmed from some form of childhood trauma. He wasn't exactly operating with two chopsticks in the sushi.

As fellow inmates, it had been our job to talk him down away from the confrontations with the wall. The staff could not have cared less. It seems that Norman had lit the town of Bellingham on fire. Norman was a serial arsonist. The savvy inmates steered clear of Norman and gave him a wide berth. It was not exactly known what he might be capable of.

Norman and I were released to the same halfway house at the same time. We had a mutual respect seeing as how we had done a stretch of time together. Most folks in the halfway house were there for what is called pre-sentencing. They'd go see the judge and get a slap on the wrist, and then come back and finish their miniscule sentences, avoiding prison altogether. Some considered it an extended vacation. The atmosphere was different for Norman. For the most part, he was no longer regarded with a wary eye. In my way of thinking this was a disadvantage. The Newbies did not know he was a potential time bomb.

A fellow housemate named Mensa would antagonize Norman repetitively and thought that it was hilarious.

"Don't fuck with Norman, or he will fuck you back," I warned.

Mensa's high-pitched response: "Dat wetod coon't fuck wit' me if he had a puthy."

He had undoubtedly learned this phrase in baby prison—juvenile detention. He must have found it hard trying to pull off being a badass with his squeaky voice and lisp.

I shrugged.

"OK, Mensa Man, if you say so," I said and left it at that.

Up to that point, Norman had cut him some slack. Mensa was unaware the slack would soon run out.

Later that night, Halloween as it so happened, I heard what sounded like the soundtrack of a high-volume horror movie that came from the direction of the TV room. But it was no movie. This was a live performance and it was horrific. Wes Craven couldn't have written a better scene. I don't know what Mensa Man had said that set Norman off, but we all heard Mensa's pleas to a distant God.

"*OH GOD—HE'TH EATING ME*!"

It was between mealtimes and Norman had a hearty appetite; he had ripped a meaty chunk out of Mensa Man's back. Coming up for air, he gave us all an award-winning Hannibal Lecter smile. For Norman, I hope it was savory and sweet. For Mensa Man, a teachable moment for sure. He had an expanded understanding of language with the new word karma. I couldn't help but feel Norman was better suited for the Big House than the halfway house.

Chapter 62
Suspicions Abound

After spending so much time inside, I had tiptoed out of prison for my first look around to see what dangers lurked beyond the razor wire. Having been surrounded by "truth tellers" (nobody acts like their word is as golden as cons) for so long, my B.S. meter was set on high. This mental recipe had served me well while in lockup considering the constant possibilities. In the free world, it was not so tasty. I had more than a little trepidation as to what the big, new, scary world had to offer me. My previous interpretation of the free world was that I could help myself to anything that was not nailed down. This time my understanding would be different.

Once back on "the scene" I had a hard time. My perception of people's intentions was a bit skewed. It was a real blow to my ego to find out they didn't always think about me. Like when I was at a Mariners baseball game and saw my probation officer. It turns out she was not on special assignment to stalk me but just another baseball fan.

I was taking a Jacuzzi at the college fitness center. I felt relaxed and refreshed until I became the focus of attention from a guy sitting across from me.

"What the fuck are you looking at," I spat.

Startled, he got out of the Jacuzzi. He was physically handicapped. I was so ashamed I couldn't look anyone in the eye for quite a while. I was still somewhat afraid of people. I felt sneaked up on, especially by waiters.

At a restaurant dinner party for my mom, I ducked into the bar to check the score of a game. As I watched, I started a long, one-sided conversation with a black dude. I got hot around the collar because I felt he had disrespected me by not responding. True, the lights were on the low side and all of his clothes, hat, and skin color were identical, as well as his drink, but I really thought he was rude … until I realized he was bronze. Cast bronze.

They put him there because they knew I would be there.

After I skulked back into the restaurant, I couldn't help but feel a little bit weird about myself.

My take-home pay in prison was obviously low. It became hard for me to fathom the real world cost of goods and services. I would walk through the organic grocery store and mutter about gilded chickens. Once while shopping for shirts, I became unraveled. A young male clerk brimming with enthusiasm approached and asked "May I help you?"

I may have been beyond help.

"You're not getting my money," I yelled.

I've always had trouble keeping my mouth shut. But, I have what I like to call European-style teeth, fairly crooked and not so white. I decided I would kill two birds with one stone by using Crest whitening strips while driving to work. With the bleach strips affixed to my teeth, I barreled down the highway daydreaming about my future as a Seattle City Councilman (which would be a prelude to my state Senate seat because I know how to fix shit). I was nearly forced off the highway by a vehicle trying to steal my lane. The pain in my ass was a throwback from Woodstock, a '60s VW van complete with flower power stickers plastered all over it. Already foaming at the mouth, I reflexively un-holstered both middle fingers and blasted him, rapid fire.

"FUCK, FUCK, FUCK, FUCK YOOOOU," I screamed.

A crimson hue started at the base of his neck and rapidly headed north. I thought his ears would burst into flames. I imagined his head as a steam whistle. He fired a volley back at me. I ducked and dodged as he let loose with his foul-mouthed barrage. I mocked him, curled my bottom lip and rubbed my eyes with my fists like a bawling baby would do. This taunt pushed him over the edge of what should have been a normal and pleasant road rage experience into borderline psychotic. For this guy, the summer of love was but a fleeting memory. Up on two wheels, he almost ran his hippy-mobile off the road as he tried to keep me away from my lane.

I win again, I thought as I finished cutting him off and drove on down the highway.

As I adapted to life outside with estrogen seeping in, I arrived at the point where I decided to put my name and phone number on the side of my truck. The signage would do double duty: advertise my business and help control my road rage. Thus began the inevitable mild-mannered, middle-aged slide into male womanhood.

Terrell had a distinctly different idea of middle-aged womanhood. I knew I had a problem when she yelled at the guy who had cut *her* off.

"Suck my dick!"

I found this shocking for an educated woman who had majored in foreign languages. I thought I was the only one in the marriage who got to have road rage ... or a dick. Was it possible she suffered from a bout of I.G.S.—Irritable Gal Syndrome—that would pass with aspirin and bed rest?

No such luck.

When we got married, I heard the pastor say, "Through thick and thin."

This episode was on "the thin" side.

I was going to need a heavy-duty seatbelt and some extra thick skin because I was in for a long ride. The more years that pass between us, the more our hormonal inversion intensifies. My wife has what seems an inexhaustible newfound well of testosterone, and I'm damned if I know what she's so angry with me about half the time.

"Whad I do, Whad I do?" I say to her, sounding like a paranoid parrot.

My wife is as beautiful as ever and I don't see a pair swingin' when I look down there, but her voice gets lower and slower while mine gets higher and faster. She claims becoming a man invigorates her. I don't much care for becoming a woman.

I cut her a lot of slack though because God's sense of humor knows no bounds when it comes to hormonal reverse polarity. As I resettled into life among the "normies," Terrell has shown me how to love, and I have rebounded nicely.

Of all the transitions I faced, getting back into the workforce proved to be one of the hardest. It was a tough job market after 9/11. *Surely I could wash dishes at IHOP*, I thought as I set out to get a job. I was deemed overqualified for the job of a hydro-ceramics technician. Talk about demoralizing.

I was adamant about answering honestly the one question always posed to job applicants: "Have you ever been convicted of a felony?" There could be no, yes, buts. It didn't matter. It can't be explained away. I stuck to my guns. A straight yes, followed by "we'll let you know." I even came clean at the temp agency. As I told my tale, the gal shoved her chair back onto two legs while she windmilled her arms so she wouldn't go over backward. She was speechless, literally couldn't talk. I thanked her and walked away mid stammer. That's the main reason I'm self-employed today.

It was why I turned to my buddy J.P. for work. He had remained a relative constant in my life and had done a stretch behind bars. He could relate.

He had gotten arrested and sent to the King County Jail for their work-release program—work by day and jail by night. As a genius entrepreneur, he thought selling the weed he smuggled into the jail would be a good venture. He got arrested again, this time inside the jail and his work-release status was revoked. What began as a one-year sentence turned into four. He was sentenced for drug sales and sent off to prison.

When he got out, he showed up to my place of employment totally ripped from the prison weight pile and the cooler full of Heinekens in the trunk of his Galaxy 500. He wore a 10-gallon cowboy hat to go along with his 10-gallon-a-day beer habit. Extreme drinking was his sport until he got sober in 1990.

He's always been a natural born athlete, big boned and unafraid. Slightly overweight now, he doesn't see it and it takes nothing away from his confidence. J.P. is often infuriating and sometimes selfish, but when it comes to parenting and helping someone get sober, nobody does it better.

For a time, he changed very little after he got sober, a wheeler-dealer and a totally over-the-top manic, draped in gold and smoking cigars. He could talk the sealskin boots off of a frozen Eskimo while bangin' the Eskimos wife. When I got out, he always had a few things going on, so he would throw some work my way, like the time he enlisted me to help build a fence. He picked up a couple guys off the streets the day before and deposited them at the job site clueless. J.P. wasn't concerned with background. He wasn't concerned with quality control either. Nor was he into laboring, He was a "manager." When I got there, they had set the fence posts. They looked like leftover trees from the Mount St. Helens blast, not exactly what I'd call plumb. After we reset and framed the posts, J.P. shot the fence boards in with a nail gun leaving one inch of nail sticking out the other side. He noticed my look of concern.

"Don't worry," he said. "It's all part of my master plan. We'll cut them off with a blow torch."

Nicely done. Ouch!

Years later, as a real estate agent J.P. called me to a potential listing to look at a small construction project. I did my diligent calculations and gave the homeowner a bid of $600. The homeowner told me had sought a bid from a guy draped in gold about two years earlier. Rather than doing any calculations, they guy waved his magic arms and declared, "Three grand."

As we left, J.P. pulled me aside and said, "that was me."

Of course, it was. I love J.P. like a brother.

Chapter 63
Photo I.D.

God threw me a bone when I was introduced to my sweetheart. We met at the church of the Episc-o-Pals. She was reading *Escape from Intimacy*, and I was reading *Struggle for Intimacy*. It's a miracle that we were able to synch up.

As we got to know each other, I felt I had to come clean. In detail, I told Terrell about my life-o-crime.

"How exciting," she said, shocking me with a positive response.

"Only for a moment," I said.

In my prior attempts at romantic relations, I teetered like a two-legged stool, unable to stand on my own. In recovery, this would be called two stepping: My life is unmanageable, and I'd like to share it with you. But now I felt ready and willing to move forward in a clean and healthy way, but Terrell had her reservations. Who can blame her?

What a catch, an ex-con at forty-two living in his sister's basement without a pot to piss in or a window to throw it out of. Somehow, despite the deck stacked against me she felt a gravitational pull. I suspected it, yet she did not know it at the time. She tried to send me packing more than once.

"This isn't going anywhere," she told me. "We're not right for each other."

"We're entering into a deeper phase of our relationship," I'd reply.

That pissed her off.

She'd look at me like I was an alien, but I was nothing if not persistent. She allowed me to keep seeing her. The woman who would become my wife had plenty of doubts about me. I knew they were legitimate. I didn't expect her to take me at face value. I needed to show not tell. I believed I had potential, and I wanted her to believe it too.

But other factors were also at play. She had manufactured concerns based on the behavior of the men that had previously been in her life. It wasn't just me she doubted when she launched in.

"We're never going to be right for each other," said the broken record.

I knew she was attracted to me and that her body responded to mine even before being intimate, but I hid my hurt until she said it one too many times. I whipped out my can of act fast and my driver's license.

"How many pictures do you see?" I asked.

"One," Terrell replied.

"That's right, one. I'm not your dad and I'm not your brother or your ex-husband. I'm that guy," I said, poking my finger on the forehead of my D.M.V. photo.

I had the added benefit of the wise council of her girlfriends who said, "Mandela was in prison," and "we don't make him pay twice."

I realize I'm no Nelson Mandela, but I'm no Charles Manson, either. She caved and gave me the chance I had been angling for. We were far enough into our relationship that she never had to try and squeeze the toothpaste back into the tube. She gave me a whirl, and we've spun a great life together for more than thirteen years.

My birds and bees equation as an adult before recovery was that sex before love equaled shame. I felt sex was a pointless and mentally exhausting endeavor where all roads lead to self-loathing. Moving through time, I confirmed it again and again and felt worse and worse about myself. The thought never occurred to me that waiting until I fell in love was optional.

Hello.

When courting my wife, she laid the ninety-day rule on me. No physical contact beyond kissing for ninety days. Rejection is protection. At first I wasn't pleased until I discovered our bodies liked each other and things were beginning to look up.

Early on, I learned my bride is a very sensitive woman, often bursting into tears for reasons unknown to me. I would look around in a panic to make sure no one saw the imaginary abuse I dished out to her. I took it personally that she cried, fearing that I'd done something wrong. As it turns out, I am not all-powerful. She was just feeling her feelings.

"Feelings, what's that?" I'd ask.

Terrell comes from a family of financial cutthroats and found it necessary to detach from them to work on her emotional self. I was still shedding my emotional prison baggage, rigid as an oak plank and void of most emotions. I hadn't yet learned how to experience my feelings. This was a great survival tool in prison and as a child growing up under the chaos of Ill Will's reign, but I learned it was no longer practical in the real world. A nice counterbalance began to take place at exactly the right time for me. My Higher Power (I call H.P.) had a plan.

Now I have three pots to piss in and about twenty windows to throw it out of. If there's any question as to how much I still love her, I just point to the fact that I accept the Victoria's Secret lunch bag she sends me off with to my construction sites. My neighbor Jackie once yelled over at me snickering "Nice bag," when she walked by. I would eat my lunch out of a Tampax box if that's what it takes.

Chapter 64
Members Only

Not one to miss an opportunity to witness a crime, I was in the right place at the right time. On my periodic quest for a healthier mind and body, I was in the YMCA Jacuzzi after a swim. The pool was a family friendly area designed to be occupied by boys and girls, men and women alike. This day it was just me and two women in the hot tub, one young, one old and a pool full of female aerobicizers. The sign next to the conveniently located hot room common area shower states, "shower before entering the Jacuzzi." A robust 65ish male read it otherwise. His interpretation was, "and don't forget to wash your sack." He dropped his version of a shock-and-awe bomb minus the awe, stripped naked, and scrub-a-dub dubbed. He showed off his rosy cheeks, which looked like twin sinister sunrises. The two women in the hot tub thought so. Both were aghast and simultaneously attempted to check out and disappear behind their hands. I, on the other hand, did not check out but checked in.

"HEEEEY ROSIE, WHAT THE FUCK," I yelled.

He turned around while the Jacuzzi sisters dropped their hands and raised their heads to focus all their attention on junior. Like a championship synchronized swim team, the aerobicizers' heads spun around in unison. The sight of Buck Naked caused them to temporarily lose motor function temporarily flailing. He pled stupidity, scurried back into his swim trunks and slithered away and left me holding the bag to apologize for my gender. He disappeared so fast you would have thought his feet were on fire.

A nice young lifeguard was assigned the super sleuth investigative duties. He asked if anyone saw this man. I hoped they didn't put him on a milk carton.

"Yeah, we all saw him. He was about 4 ½ inches tall, was wearing a turtle neck and a helmet, had one eye and was pink," I said.

The lifeguard gave me the weirdest look, as if he was going to vomit before he soldiered on with the task at hand.

"Does anyone know his name?" he asked.

I threw Flash Johnson out there for the hell of it.

I hope that's not what I have to look forward to in ten years. I believe it was an honest mistake. Hopefully, it is not one he will make again. Could have happened to anyone on a nude beach in Amsterdam. I'm especially glad Super Sleuth didn't have me identify him in a lineup. My thoughts for safe travels were with him as he made his way to the Canadian border. I believe this event will stay with him longer than it stayed with any of us, but I doubt he'll be telling it to his grandchildren.

In this second chapter of my life, I try to give people the benefit of the doubt. In the spirit of paying it forward, I tried to help another ex-con who was just getting out of prison. I used to have a bad habit of trying to replicate myself. I am learning that not everyone is interested in being me. Go figure. This ex-con was no exception. Not only did he not want to be me, but more importantly, he didn't exactly subscribe to my preferred program of recovery, which should have been a red flag. He did keep a low profile. One of the hard and fast rules while on supervised release is not to knowingly associating with another ex-convict. I was taking a risk by even trying to help him get on the right path.

Vicki had sold me a nice little car for a great deal. A Dodge Colt Vista Wagon with a 1.4-litre motor. I had built a box for it and filled it with roofing debris, a makeshift truck. Sounds like something Ill Will would do. I bought a real truck and no longer needed it. I turned it over to ConEx on a payment plan while holding the title. With three payments down and three to go I got a call from my probation officer.

"Your car was found parked in front of a motel in Eugene, Oregon," he said.

He came into this information after he was called by Mr. ConEx's probation officer. I came clean and was cut some slack. Lesson learned.

Seems Mr. Ex binged on coke and wandered off from the car to peer into neighboring motel windows until he got arrested. I called the motel and gave them the short version of "my car was stolen." They promised not to tow it. I took the train down and retrieved the car, which was mechanically sound but thrashed on the inside. It had not only become his home on wheels but a mobile shooting gallery, with the telltale signs of cracked behavior. Full of pizza boxes, dirty socks, booze bottles and spent syringes. Cleaning it was a grim reminder of how fleeting sanity is for some who make the wrong choices. My resolve strengthened.

"Better him than me," I said out loud to myself, to make sure I heard it. "I'm not going back."

After a thorough cleaning, I was on the road.

Back home, I learned more about my wayward reclamation project who beat his now ex-girlfriend out of six hundred dollars for the down payment on the car and spent it on drugs. She was "normie" and not involved in the sordid junky lifestyle. She had no idea what was on the horizon. I did get a chance to pay it forward. She needed a vehicle and only had the amount still owed on mine. Credited for the three payments made, she got herself a car for the remaining balance. Problem solved, and all parties were happy. Except one.

Thankfully, many of the times I try to pay it forward turn out to be more meaningful.

Ed was seventeen years sober and on daily kidney dialysis when I met him. I'd see him at various mutual nighttime meeting places around town. He made an announcement that he had gotten on the kidney donor list. The prospect of him being free of the dialysis machine was exciting news to everyone he told. He had been going for a very long time.

Not a week later doctors found cancerous tumors on his liver, and they took him off the list. Their best diagnosis was a couple of months to live. He took it better than everyone else. Ed was a bachelor, didn't drive and had no family. We lived in the same neighborhood, so I was the natural choice to help out where I could. I was going to school and working only part-time, so I made myself available. Once I took him grocery shopping. We had spent an awful long time in the store and yet not a single item had found its way into his basket.

"What's the matter, Ed?" I asked. "Don't you know how to cook?"

"I'm learning," he said.

We opted for quick and easy. Back at his apartment I heated up some Campbell's tomato soup.

"Man, that's good," he said.

That simple statement really affected me.

He went downhill fast. I took him to the hospital on a Friday and sat bedside with him until Sunday evening when he died. He was in his early sixties. He had done a good stretch in prison and had turned his life around. He died sober. I had seen death but never gone through the dying process with someone before. It was sad and beautiful and an experience I'll never forget.

Chapter 65
La Cucaracha

Vicki put me up after my release from the halfway house. Eventually, she made me leave her nest. I was a little bit scared. I soon got into the groove and enjoyed my little flat. A lot of characters lived in the neighborhood, and the buildings were tightly spaced.

Despite the squalor and the cockroaches, my bachelor pad was the one and only time in my life that I lived alone, or at least without any other humans. It was a milestone for me.

I can cook hamburgers, spaghetti and eggs, but this was not always the case. As a kid, I would celebrate my heritage and drizzle vegetable oil on my Wonder bread just like a real Frenchmen. Things were sparse. One day when I was about twelve my mom quit cooking. She was done. I was forced to learn fast as she gave me a box of Hamburger Helper, where the helping hand has only a middle finger. This drove home her point. I didn't learn too much. Now, a spry college student of forty-two, I left a pot of pinto beans on the stove in my third floor flat. I was sitting the in lobby when someone entered the building and said, "Ooh, smells like ass."

I bolted up to the third floor and extinguished the disgusting mess, relieved that the fire department was not en route.

Parking was a challenge on Pill Hill, a name associated with the proximity of many hospitals. I needed some magic pills for my disease of car auction-itis. Once I moved onto Pill Hill, I would spend a lot of time moving my three cars from one two-hour spot to the next. When I rushed off to class, I knew I would have to spend plenty of time later looking for where I'd parked them all. I'd begin the hunt at the far reaches, blocks away and go round and round, working my way inward hoping I would run into one of my cars before the hungry tow trucks swallowed them up. I felt relief when one of the fuel pumps went out in my Volvo. I gave my car to the Center for the Blind hoping they wouldn't get into a wreck.

I lived on the top floor of the 1920s three-story apartment building with an alley in between and another one just like it right outside my window. Across the alley I would see Guitarzan, an Iggy Pop lookalike nod off from what I suspected was heroin (seeing as how the smoldering skin from the cigarette burning between his fingers wouldn't stir his slumber nor would his guitar that was feeding back against the ever present Marshall Stack amplifier).

I would yell "Heeeeey, HEEEEY."

No response.

Jimi Hendrix playing the Star Spangled Banner had nothing on him. He didn't hear me nor did he hear the pit bull that lived in the alley while constantly talking to Guitarzan's amplifier.

Terrell had five non-negotiables for a man when we met. 1) Geographically available 2) Passionate about his work 3)

Non-smoker 4) Close to the same age… and believe it or not… 5) Wears cuff links. Huh?!

I had worn handcuffs. So I won on a technicality.

So, it shouldn't have surprised me that she wouldn't sit on the green corduroy sofa I bought for $30 off the street and carried it into to my third-floor apartment. She wouldn't even come over until I got rid of it. I ended up having no furniture.

I owe a debt of gratitude to the infestation of cockroaches that occurred in my bachelor pad. I am oddly nostalgic about cockroaches. I too know what it's like being a diseased insect that only showed myself after dark. But as they overrun my little pad, my wife-to-be felt prompted to invite me to co-habitat with her. She felt a little sorry for me.

Nostalgia has its limits. I don't miss it anymore.

Terrell soon became introduced to the strange connection I had to the world when Jimmy the Shoe from prison showed up to spend some time with us. He and his new gal friend came to Seattle to see me and mine. We had just bought our first house.

Jimmy was a long-suffering heroin addict who year after year chased the bag around the prison yard and paid every penny he ever owed. He would sidle up to me like Walter Brennan, sounding half drunk and say "Wassup, dog." He was well respected and a stand-up guy in every way. I liked the shit out of that guy. I shot recovery barbs at him at every opportunity only to be told "maybe tomorrow." He went back to prison on a violation after his release. Tomorrow had finally arrived. He admitted defeat and started hanging with the winners and against all odds, stayed sober.

I chartered a boat and took him salmon fishing on Puget Sound. He had never been fishing. I caught a mud shark, and he caught two beautiful silver salmon.

He said, "I don't eat that shit, here" handing me the filets.

He was a biscuits and gravy kind of a guy.

Later, Terrell was treating me kind of chilly.

"What's wrong?" I asked.

"I just had a surreal experience, I found a black and white tuxedo thong complete with a bow tie on its crotch clinging to our dryer," she said.

"Well it's not mine," I said defensively," I'm a boxer kind of guy, you know that."

Putting our investigative skills to work, we determined Jimmy's main squeeze had done a load of laundry and left it behind. I gained a little credibility that day. It was still early, and I needed all I could get.

I grew through these tests, but they kept coming. After my release it seems I started getting one test after another. I came home one day to discover a suitcase safe on my property busted open and loaded with goodies. Passports, driver's licenses, gold coins, rings, silver ingots and foreign currency. I invited the police into my house to retrieve it. I had never done that before.

I also found a wallet full of cash in Lowes parking lot. Some habits die hard. I did count it, more than six hundred bucks. Then the new habit kicked in. I turned it in. The manager thanked me profusely. Still later I found a briefcase full of credit cards. It just keeps coming. My H.P. has a sense of humor, it seems.

Chapter 66
Tomato Paste

We were a relatively new couple, so I felt I had to pull out all the stops to market myself as potential husband material. Cooking, which I am now good at, was a go-to activity that would help put me in the best possible light. Most of the time it worked well.

I blame the gnarly Chinese-American buffet that had been sitting under heat lamps from the day before. I would never cop to problems with my cooking. But whatever it was, Terrell and I were both in the kitchen, and I was trying mightily to keep it all together as my stomach roiled from apparent food poising. I was making a salad when I felt something a little too moist.

"I think I just dropped a tomato down my pants," I said.

This would have been difficult to accomplish seeing as how my shirt was tucked in. Upon further investigation, that abstract thought died on the vine. Seepage. I was under the impression I had about forty more years before I started the process of shitting in my pants.

Oh, the horror.

Terrell saw the concern on my face. She asked if there was anything she could do.

Run out for a package of Huggies, I thought but bit my tongue while squeezing my innards.

Driven by shame, I made a beeline to the bathroom wondering how long I could camp out there before she would just go away. I knew our relationship was now, finally, doomed.

When she enquired whether I was alright from the other side of door sometime later, I let the scat out of the bag hoping she would take that information with her to the grave. Misery does love company, I found out. Apparently she was as sick as I. This wasn't a deal breaker. Her response was loving and compassionate. It made me want to shit myself all over again.

Perhaps against her better judgment, Terrell eventually came to agree with me that we were "right" for each other. She even said. "I do."

As we gathered to say our vows, I looked around our venue at a wide network of healthy, stable friends and loved ones that materialized since my release from prison. I had no idea that this would be the case. There were more than 100 people at my wedding. A grand total of four had been at my sentencing. Please and thank-you only goes so far when you're knocking down banks like bowling pins. Like an unsalted potato chip, I was considered unsavory. Now I'm told I'm a little bit salty and crusty.

When sharing parts of my story, some people take a step back but then two steps forward leading with their ear.

"You don't look like a bank robber," I hear often.

"You should have seen me way back when," I say.

I understand the incessant glorification of drug use by most of those in prison. They know nothing else. It's the sum of their experience. I'm fortunate that with a lot of help, I've moved beyond that mindset. There was a time I was right there with them. My life is big and getting bigger all the time. The free gift of love is out there for the taking as long as I give it back.

E.E.

Chapter 67
Bloodletting

After our wedding, my lovely wife and I reviewed destination options for our honeymoon. Paris was at the top of the list but for financial reasons it would have to wait until later. Our second choice was to drive to San Francisco.

After hitting the road, I realized all was not right with the world. In my mind, what was a minor muscle strain mutated into broken ribs and quickly morphed into eminent death. I've never been kicked by a mule, but I was convinced I had been visited by one in my sleep and that my organs were hemorrhaging inside of me. So much for the romantic, leisurely scenic drive. My new bride informed me that we did see some lovely blurry sights while barreling down the highway at 85 miles-an-hour on our way to a bay area hospital that was within our insurance coverage network.

My medical insurance was not so stellar, so the 1-800 number directed us to the emergency room of the Not-So-Stellar Medical Center where they made their diagnosis: I had shingles of the non-construction variety. That explained why I felt half-bad, as it only affects one side of your body. I remembered hearing chronic snivelers tell tales of woe about what I thought was the imaginary pain of shingles. I had considered the sufferers all a bunch of weenies. I was mortified to realize that I too had entered into a state of unadulterated weenie-dom. This shingles business fucking hurt.

The ER staff stuffed me into a Magnetic Resonance Imaging tube to appease my suspicions and get a gander at my insides. The blood tech, my man Phlebo who seemed fairly competent, hooked me up for a draw and left me alone with my illnesses, real and imagined. I took some comfort in the thought of quickly healing and getting on to the big city to enjoy my honeymoon. I dreamed of visiting the Levi and Ghirardelli Chocolate factories, just like Willie Wonka when I felt a tickling sensation on my arm. I looked down, and there was a pool of blood on the floor the size of my dining room table with a leaf in. I had no idea my body held so much blood.

"HEEEEEYY!" I yelled at the top of my lungs.

My man Phlebo came running. Phlebo took one look and hollered.

"AAHHHH!"

He threw his arms up in the air flapping in an apparent attempt to fly out of the room. I did not find his response a real confidence builder. The widow's peak should have been a dead giveaway. He was back in a flash with an oversized string mop. He slung that mop back and forth wildly through the puddle of blood like he was swabbing the deck of a reeling ship. Jackson Pollack style paintings soon appeared on the walls.

"Oh, my God, oh, my God, oh, my God," he repeated with each pass of the mop.

"Just curious. What the fuck does that mean?" I asked.

I felt little woozy myself, but I could tell I had nothing on Phlebo. He was beyond queasy and was quickly becoming a very light-skinned brother. I asked him if he needed a doctor. I am pretty sure he thought he needed a lawyer right about then.

Sitting in the ER lab trying to recover, I reviewed lessons learned and felt that I had been duped by my childhood geography teacher. I'd always thought Transylvania was an Eastern European region, not a suburb of San Francisco.

After declining his generous offer of a Transylvania transfusion, I informed Phlebo that he ought to be glad my ferocious, peri-menopausal wife didn't get to witness the bloodletting because I wouldn't have had enough strength left in me to protect him. I escaped with some of my blood still inside me and let bygones be bygones. With the help of some medication for my shingles and a couple of days rest, I went on to resurrect what turned into a spectacular honeymoon.

The hospital bill had arrived home before I did. I didn't have to wait long to find out the cost of donating so much blood. As it turns out, it was quite expensive.

One of the highlights of our honeymoon was a visit to a world-famous Wok Shop in San Francisco's Chinatown. We seemed to enter the shop right in the middle of a verbal shit-storm-slash-temper-tantrum between the owner—who on this day lacked in the area of social grace—and her loyal employee, who at 100 decibels claimed over 25 years of loyal service. We stepped up to the register with our coveted giant wok and prepared to get hit by a flying rice steamer or two. With every expletive that flew out of the "loyal" employee's mouth, a nifty new cooking gadget would fly into our shopping bag.

"Here, you'll be needing one of these, no charge."

"You stupid fu****g bi##h, I hate you," the owner howled from the background.

"No kitchen should be without one of these, no charge," the employee said in a voice now as pleasant as a kindergarten teacher.

She served up her brand of justice one utensil at a time. By the time she had cussed herself out, I needed another set of arms to carry all my new stuff.

"Have a nice day, and please come again," she said as we hauled our surprising wedding present away.

As we adjusted to married life, I learned Terrell has 18th-century European sensibilities. Mine are more of the 1849 San Francisco variety. I'm a Levis kind of a guy. I can make an effort on a special occasion, although begrudgingly. I buy clothes, wear them once, hang them up, decide they look stupid, that I hate them, brood over them and stuff them into the vast recesses of our closet never to be seen again… until she pulls the article out and exclaims, "you never wear this, I'm giving it away."

That's when I throw a fit.

"Nooooooo! I like it. I'm gonna wear it someday,"

Poof, then it's gone. She isn't buying it any more than I was wearing it.

When we shopped for a sofa, Terrell wanted some high-backed, Elizabethan nonsense. I put my foot down. Or rather, she made a concession and we got one made from a pasture full of cows. In short, we figured out how to navigate across the vast gulf of our different life experiences. I've seen every masterpiece theater offering from the last thirty years. I watch, and I sigh and I sigh. I thought I was gonna have to change my name to Giles, for crying out loud. I even went to the opera once. Good Lord, man! But, she's seen every prison movie ever made. We'll watch a particularly lively heist, and she'll say "You owe me two Jane Austens."

Her major in college was a foreign language. When we met, I spoke a foreign language: Prison Yard. We had a party, and I made a sign on our French doors indicating "Drinks–n- stuff."

"Absolutely not," was her response in clear English to my fancy sign.

Like random drug testing in prison, my wife does random clothes washing.

"You wore this and hung it up," she said with her nose scrunched.

"Only for a couple of hours," I'll say.

Poof, gone.

I'm not allowed to do laundry, so I can't complain. Previously, my new Levi's turned everything we owned blueish-gray, hooray, my favorite colors. Not to mention all the drill bits, driver tips and crap I leave in my pockets that shred everything in their path. The old washer was not a front loader. She got tired of me ripping the sleeves off her blouses when unloading, so we bit the bullet and bought the front loader.

Another fancy gadget in my new-shared domesticated world is the De Longi Easy Serve Espresso Maker, which came free courtesy of Jeff Besos. After crappy instant coffee for so many years, this is heaven. Amazon offered this bad boy at half price for $100, so I bought it. Two days after receiving it, I received another one. I called and explained the situation and the helpful customer service pros sent me a shipping ticket to send it back. Three days after shipping it back I received a refund for $100. I once again called customer service and they told me to, "just keep the money. It's too complicated." I gotta wonder how Besos became a billionaire.

Chapter 68
Reconciliation Not

Bless my sister Pam for keeping my location secret.

Ill Will sent a message wishing me well.

"Tell him he owes me money."

He needed money because all he had to do was send it to that Nigerian official so the paperwork could be completed to release his millions from winning the Nigerian lotto, even though he had never set foot on the African continent.

I know I wasn't always working with two oars in the water and realize there are some mental health issues in my family history, but when you get out of bed on Christmas Eve and make yourself two sandwiches from the Christmas ham like Ill Will did at Pam's house, it's a clear indication of the depth of his issues. I choose to get help on a daily basis. The world is a safer place because of it. Ill Will, on the other hand, stuck to his guns and self-medicated with alcohol, gambling, and bad behavior until the day he died. A month before he passed away, he had a burst of generosity. Vicki got a phone call from Ill Will. He asked her if he could borrow $5,000 to buy some land so he could leave her something when he died. What a plan, what a guy. On his death bed, when offered guaranteed salvation during last rights, he declined saying, "I wasn't buying yesterday, and I'm not buying today."

We went on a total of two family vacations when I was a kid growing up. Ill Will had a habit of showing up unannounced to this or that so-called friend's house with family in tow expecting to be fed and entertained. I think they were too afraid of him to set him straight.

One such excursion was a cross-country trip. We flew from Seattle to St. Louis, rented a car, and drove to Michigan, Florida and Tennessee in 1975 where I met my dad's father for the only time. I was fifteen. He said "ugh." He grunted. He never said one word to me, or Ill Will, nor was he happy to see us. We were there for a week. I was miserable. My cousins in Memphis were in a punk band. I bought a bag of weed with the money I found in the bathroom of the crappy Greek restaurant where I got sick in Florida. Praise be to Jah, the vacation was not a total bust, other than its one of the few memories I have of Ill Will's attempt at family relationships.

Before Ill Will died, I took a pass at attempting reconciliation. Ill Will left my life consistent with the way he lived his life: largely absent and unchanged.

Chapter 69
How Do You Handle A Hungry Dog?

One of my most haunting regrets was that I gave away my dog Tork. As a living amends, I rescued Zinc, just like my wife had done for me. We've both never had it so good. When I got him, he was fifty-seven pounds of suspicion and bad attitude. As a Norwegian Elkhound, his fighting weight should have been around seventy-five pounds.

There isn't much of an elk problem in Seattle unless you consider the Mariners Moose. Zinc made up for the lack. He would mean mug ceramic foo dogs or look sideways and growl at plastic bags that blew down the street or anything else that presented a perceived direct threat. Like a true badass, he would ignore all real direct threats, like a neighborhood dog I call Hannibal. Hannibal wore what looks like an old-timey catcher's mask that encases his head on his walks. He probably eats liver and fava bean dog food with a nice Chianti. They ought to wheel him around strapped to a hand truck to complete the comparison. But Zinc doesn't even give him a glance, which adds to Hannibal's madness.

Zinc loves me. Once when a dog and owner approached, Zinc took preemptive measures and peed on my leg to let the other dog know "he's mine, don't even think about it." The dog owner said, "Wow, I've never seen that before."

I wasn't even mad. I'll take love and belonging however it's expressed.

Zinc's a street snacker. He dives into the bushes and comes out with a prize, and I'm a softy when it comes to table scraps. Zinc, also known as the Pan Handler, started to put on weight. Sixty, sixty-four, seventy-two, eighty-three, hike. He started resembling a giant furry Idaho russet with legs. He had no neck. He started to waddle, and I felt extremely bad.

My sister-in-law brought over a special mystery treat, and Zinc went *crazy*. She said it was a sun-dried, wood-smoked pizzle.

"What's a pizzle?" I asked.

"A cow penis, you know, a bully stick," she replied.

Knowing that cows didn't have penises I realized somewhere out in a pasture these bulls were missing theirs, with new names like Daisy and Buttercup to choose from. Some identity issues were going to have to be worked out. A support group may be in order.

Zinc made light work of the coveted treat. I was assured that dogs don't have to be gay to enjoy them.

He had a habit of walking backward up to one extra-fancy row of box hedges and top them off with his gnarly nuggets. The tightness of the topiary allowed the Zinc McNuggets to stand proud like hood ornaments on display for all to admire. I was tempted to lacquer them.

Elkhounds take down their prey by eviscerating the moose's genitals. Believing that no good deed should go unpunished, he tried that technique on a German shepherd service animal. Zinc was possibly still sore over the occupation of Norway. I was partly to blame, I guess. He had gone rogue as a result of my drum practice. This was his commentary on my rudimentary skill level. It was a truly ugly scene, the one and only time I've seen him go totally over the edge. Zinc circled around and dove in like a great white shark, trying to get hold of Adolf's junk. After I tackled him in the street with expletive's flying all round and the German's package still intact, the earth still spun. Back at the bunker in anticipation of my lawsuit, I immediately hung up my sticks, enrolled him in anger management classes and weight watchers. Now, at seventy-six pounds, he's the sweetest, healthiest dog the world has ever known.

Still not devoid of problems, he has progressed from sucking on his pillow to humping it, then destroying his bed and immediately going into shame. As a neutered dog, he may recognize that his sexual overtures will never be returned. There was a time that I could totally relate.

Chapter 70
Growth

As part of their due diligence, the wily staffers at the King County Jail evaluate the mental state of every inmate. Years earlier, I had been no exception. As their attractive shrink came in to talk to me, things were looking up. I looked at her thinking, "I wonder if she is willing to write to me while I'm in prison." Come to find out her personal inquiry was not a come on, but carefully designed to see if I had the propensity to harm myself. It was a crushing realization.

Fast-forward eleven years, the same woman became my college professor. I encountered yet another realization. I discovered I was a good student. Seeing as how I dropped out of high school in need of just one credit, the idea that I would be a good student was almost unfathomable. I didn't take into consideration that my head was no longer swimming in a sea of T.H.C. I set out to become a Chemical Dependency Specialist. A noble cause and one many ex-junkies pursue. I excelled in school, getting this grant and that (partly because no one else applied) and earned a 3.96 cumulative G.P.A. Not bad for the oldest guy in the class.

I climbed my way on to the National Dean's List. I received a letter from the Almighty Education muckety mucks addressed to my mother, saying, "Mrs. Piotter," (that would be my seventy-eight-year-old mother) "Due to your son's stellar academics, he has been invited to join a group of other" smart ass mother fuckers "on an archeological dig in China, you must be so proud."

I showed it to my mom.

"You're not goin' to China," she said.

I relented.

"OK, Mom."

This was about the time of her cataract surgery. She was looking pretty cool, just like Roy Orbison. I couldn't go anyway because I was still on probation and couldn't leave the state of Washington.

I interned as a co-leader for groups with addiction and mental health issues at a duel diagnostic treatment center. The management of the mental health side of the equation felt I was a danger to the poor defenseless court ordered meth heads and criminals. I got fired from my volunteer job, which put me three credits shy of my degree. Instead I graduated with a B.F.D., thus, repeating my lifecycle as a chronic dropout. It ended up being a blessing in disguise. I didn't have the tact, temperament or steely resolve to navigate that career anyway.

Thanks, H.P.

It shames me to admit it, but ten years ago, well into recovery from drugs and alcohol, I caught the auction bug and was sick for about a year before I snapped out my Ill Will impersonation. When Publishers Clearing House would send me e-mails about my guaranteed $5,000 a week for life, I felt plenty confident that it was a personal message and that

I would be meeting Ed McMahon very soon. I responded to every one of those e-mails. It became a non-paying twenty hours a week job, an investment in my future. Then there was the used Rolex I bought online when my wife was out of town, and my furnace was out of commission. Yeah, that Rolex would solve all my problems. Upon arrival, it didn't look so shiny, it didn't keep time, it didn't keep me warm, neither did my wife for quite some time after. I consider this thinking a blood-borne disease and definitely behavior that needed to be addressed. Some are sicker than others. That would be me, again.

It took no less than the death of Ed McMahon before I could get a grip on my financial reality. I gave up on the idea that I would be the recipient of $5,000 a week for life. I was already twelve years sober, but my relationship with money is complicated. Oh, how I thought I had hit the jackpot when fresh out of prison for bank robbery up popped the banks showering me with credit card offers. I had stumbled onto another form of bank robbery, only this time legal. I still can't process who was more stupid: me for taking them or them for offering. Eventually, I grew up and learned how the whole thing worked. I realized I couldn't borrow my way into prosperity. I'm happy to say I've amended my behavior. I am credit card free. My experience with something for nothing had cost me way too much over time.

Once I stopped focusing on easy money, I realized I wasn't too bad at earning money. I had quickly moved away from J.P.'s type of work and started my own contracting business that grew, as did my reputation. Terrell and I rebuilt every inch of our home and with it finding yet another revenue stream. We run a legitimate summer vacation rental business out of our home. We live in the completely separate lower level mother-in-law apartment and rent out the beautiful top floor, which helps us to realize the fruits of our labors from our seemingly endless remodel. I was initially against it. As I've said, Terrell's smarter than me. She also tends to win these debates, so despite my objections we rented our place out.

It's been a success, with each year better than the last. Seattle has become quite a tourist destination in the summertime. Initially paranoid about the imminent damage to our home, I'm more laid back about it after that has proven to not be the case. Groups of four come for three days to a week or more and cram in as much fun as time would allow them. We've even had return clients. Jiz Parker came twice. He left behind an impressive wad on our bed two years in a row. Not bad for a guy in his 60s. This is our bed eight months of the year, so it prompted us to purchase a liquid-proof bed condom. Just wipe 'em down, guaranteed. Oh, the life of an innkeeper.

You can tell a lot about a person by cleaning up after them or by where they shop for groceries, for that matter. We have two options: Sar's market or Pacific Coast Cooperative Natural Market. When asked where a grocery store is, I don't send them to a store named after a disease. This has the added benefit of quality bounty left behind. People leave a fair amount of booze behind as well. I forget, people do some drinking on vacation, boxes of wine etcetera. My wife and I don't drink, so we've become the beer fairies to our neighbors leaving the gifts on their porch.

We've had many international guests. A guy named Shin from Japan, a fast-talking, chain-smoking businessman arrived during a rare Seattle heat wave. With no available air conditioning, he battened down the hatches, closing all doors and windows with wife and teenage son safely locked inside. He would wheel and deal on the phone in his staccato Japanese. Concerned I'd create an international incident when they all suffocated to death, I went up to ask if he would like the use of a fan.

He replied "No, no fan vewy comfobo."

These people went nowhere their entire visit.

I had just bought an Electro Lux washing machine to go along with our Bonnaroo dryer, but Mrs. Shin apparently used neither when she did the laundry. She had a makeshift clothesline strung up all over our house with reams of laundry drying. Did she wash it in the tub?

A day before they were to leave, we heard a vigorous heated conversation from the hot house up above. Then silence. They made their escape and, poof, were gone. I went up to assess the damage. Other than snot smears at teenage Japanese nose level all the way around the windows, our sturdy house was still standing. I imagined Shin Jr.'s face pressed against the windows looking out at what could have been if only he could have escaped the clutches of his warden dad.

Been there, buddy, I thought.

Piotter 316

Chapter 71
You Sexy Beast

At times, I am still surprised when I have normal interactions. Life among the "normies" can be pretty good, like the time Vicki and her wife Debra offered Terrell and me the use of their timeshare condo on the Oregon Coast. This is one of the perks of being a non-using, free and trustworthy, sober dope fiend brother.

I had always heard about the Sea Lion Caves in Oregon, a minor tourist attraction the world over. Their advertising tagline invites guests to "Wonder and Enchantment." Apparently, there was something special about them, and I aimed to find out. We decided to stop on our way to Newport.

When we arrived, Terrell and I finally witnessed the big deal, which wasn't at all what we might have expected. We were greeted by an abundance of station wagons in the parking lot and offers for guided tours. Good wholesome family fun.

With excitement brewing in the elevators on the way down through the rock formation, I caught a telltale whiff. Worried, I stole a quick glance down to check the soles of my shoes for the ill effects of a misplaced step. I was not alone. Other people checked their shoes as well. Soon an equally "wondrous" noise joined the smells. Very impressive.

What we saw was a curiosity. I had seen animal porno magazines disguised as science as a child, but this was my first live performance on a grand scale. At a glance, it looked like a snow-capped mountain, but these creatures were residents of a guano-covered, Rock of Fornication, which rose up out of the infected waters. They took part in a beastly sea lion fuck fest while bellowing at a ridiculous volume. They were like well seal-oiled machines going at it like their lives depended on it. It was an assault on the senses, awesome and disgusting at the same time. If their flippers were longer, the males would have been beating their chests like King Kong. I guess I was expecting frolicking with giant beach balls. The gulls were in the mix too, seriously pissing the sea lions off, flitting around as if sayings, "Don't mind me, carry on, pardon me, terribly sorry."

I looked at my wife through sad eyes and thought, "Man, I gotta eat more fish."

This was truly a stain on the ocean.

Nearby Little Johnny the Voyeur was transfixed.

"Mommy, Mommy, what are they doing?" he asked.

With eyes wide and momentarily transfixed herself, she snapped out of it.

"Well, Johnny, they're playing sea doctor."

An emergency response geared to quench a six-year-old's thirst for knowledge.

It was a surreal experience watching these sex machines making sure there would be future generations of little Johnny voyeurs littering the landscape. It was like The Mutual of Gomorra's Wild Kingdom. But what else are they going to do on a shit-covered rock? Their options would be limited.

There were no "Warning Animals Fucking" signs, or "Animal Porn May Traumatize Young Children," or even "Side Effects May Include arousal and Shame," but, then again, this was progressive Oregon. I wondered what they'd be selling in the gift shop.

Since Vicki and Debra now reside in Oregon, making the trek down to visit them had become something of a Thanksgiving tradition. Terrell, my mom and I arrived the night before to subdued but sincere fanfare. Despite the coming respite, Vicki's job as a mail carrier wore her out. Neither rain, nor snow, nor heat, nor gloom of night, stayed my sister from the swift completion of her appointed rounds, delivering the mail each day on foot. By the time we'd arrive, we'd have a hot meal then she'd be off to bed, with nary a conversation said.

This Thanksgiving had promise. I had previously attended a Thanksgiving that was a very different scene altogether. It was sterile, antiseptic. The host had everything prepared when we arrived, but there was no smell. She said, "Oh, I don't cook," and proceeded to serve up individual seal a meal boil-o-bags with all-in-one Thanksgiving dinners. She outdid prison. Our tradition with Vicki and Debra started the next year. I looked forward to conversation, the cooking, and the slow warm glow of tryptophan, as well as pie, football and the cutthroat Christmas ornament swap.

Here's the deal: We all had to bring a wrapped ornament and put it in the pile. Everyone drew a number, which indicated his or her spot in line. Take one unopened from the pile, or take one away from someone else. Last was the place to be. The Eugene clan was my sister Vicki, Debra, Debra's folks, cousins, brothers, nieces, and nephews. A total about fifteen, so it could get lively. Kleenex and Band-Aids should always be available during the mayhem.

My wife and I brought what I considered the coolest ornament I'd ever seen, a little man with a helmet inside of a rocket ship, made entirely of hand-blown glass. My wife had attachment issues and did not want to give it up. On the drive down my mom said to her, "If I get it, I'll give it back to you."

As it happened, the Rocket Man traveled some distance through space, circled the living room and made many stops along the way. Little Gabriel, the youngest of the nephews, went second-to-last and went gaga over the rocket man. Mom was last up.

"I'll take that," she said and snatched the coveted ornament away from little angel Gabriel's clutches before he knew what hit him. Then he started to wail.

On the road home, my mother presented Terrell with her prize. I got blisters from patting myself on the back while I lectured Mom on the subject of child trauma and relayed what a dirty stunt that was she had pulled back there.

"I'm just trying to be a better person," I told Mom, explaining how I would have never taken the Rocket Man from a baby.

"How does you tellin' me what to do, make you a better person?" she asked.

Excellent question and one I've yet to find an answer for.

E.E.

Chapter 72
The Pharaoh of Greenwood

❝My boyfriend is a hunter, and he'll be home soon," a relatively well-known female meteorologist told me.

It was a disturbing statement that made sense as I looked at a stuffed 300-pound Montana bighorn sheep standing in a custom-built pen in the middle of the weather gal's living room. It looked like a glorified cat litter box minus the kitty roca. The failed attempt at recreating the bighorn's natural environment contained sand, a few fake shrubs and the fence, which I considered akin to installing a seatbelt in a coffin. I damn near needed a plastic surgeon and a car jack to ratchet my dropped jaw back into position when I saw the sheep.

The house was a smallish rambler. From the street, nothing about it arose suspicion. Everything looked copacetic. Inside though, Ramses, as I decided to call the stuffed sheep, was the focal point. Absent from her was any indication that something was amiss, but it was not lost on me. This household had tangible issues.

Ramses had a determined look on his face, and although frozen in time, he appeared ready to knock the shit out of anyone who could inadvertently recharge his batteries. I admired his courage and pondered that the sheep never knew he was just one jammed gun away from victory. Then maybe he'd have mounted the boyfriend and the weather gal's greeting to me would have sounded like, "My boyfriend *was* a hunter, and he's *never* coming home."

Even though she was quite attractive, there was nothing untoward on my part for her to threaten me with her hunter boyfriend's arrival. I wasn't there on a cervix call. I was there on a plumbing call to fix a leaky pipe. Somehow her tone made me feel as if I'd made a big mistake. Regret washed over me. I am a contractor who works on houses, not other guy's girlfriends, a point I was prepared to make clear if and when Davy Crockett, the still mythical hunter, arrived home. I'm usually pretty good about working under a deadline, but the thought of Davy blasting his way through the door in camouflage khakis and the fact that I'm an Aries, the zodiac's ram, made me a little shaky. Me and Ramses being kindred spirits and all, left me thinking that there may also be room in that pen for me if I didn't get the leak fixed.

I frequented the local taxidermy shop often when I was a child, which filled me with a combination of shock and awe for the animals and trepidation for the shop owner. Those memories made me even more wary. This was supposed to be bleeding-heart Seattle. You may sight an occasional trophy fish on the wall.

As a child, I was equally disturbed by Bobo the gorilla, a former occupant of Woodland Park Zoo. Bobo's favorite past time was throwing shit at the Plexiglas cage and threatening to kill me. After dying of old age, Bobo was stuffed and motionless at the Seattle Museum of History and Industry where he wouldn't be throwing shit at anyone.

In short, when it comes to man vs. animal, I'm Team Animal.

Maybe the hunter just waited for Ramses to die of old age before bagging him. Maybe he would wait for me to die of old age too, which seemed to be happening at an accelerated rate as my mind raced around in frenetic chaos. My mind redlined as I heard the hunter arrive. Like a slow-moving, high-pressure system, the hunter mumbled his way into the house right on cue, brimming with a truckload of negative vibes. He looked a little pasty, probably due to not getting outside much other than when he was blowing away God's defenseless creatures in their natural habitat. He shook hands with a dead person's hand, ice cold and with the same response, none at all.

Not only did he have a ram parked in the living room, there was one parked in the drive as well: A modified, useless Dodge Ram truck with no bed and gigantic tires that require a step ladder to get up into it. With the promise of a larger payload, The commercials for these trucks appealed to those suffering from erectile dysfunction.

It made me want to say, "Nice truck, sorry about your penis," as I shook his limp grip.

(As I write this, I should probably be worried about retaliation. The hunter packs heat after all. I'm hoping that reading isn't one of his long suits.)

The Chief Meteorologist and the Hunter retreated into the dark recesses of their house of horrors leaving me with a drip that could not be stopped and a worry over the diabolical Hellfire scheme they might send raining down on me.

I finished my work under the scrutiny of the ram's two glass eyes and a perpetual scowl. The wheels between my ears couldn't have spun any faster. While gingerly packing out my tools and skulking away from the hunting grounds, I had a premonition.

"Not a snowball's chance in Hell of any sunshine happening up in here."

The joys of residential contracting are still a constant in my life, more so as I grow comfortable with myself.

"So what happened since I left?"

It was only one hour but a legitimate question from a recent client painfully concerned with the value of his dollar. Perhaps, in the past I'd get anxious and worry about losing the job. But when life works, it affords you some flexibility. Just like cream, my smart retort rose to the top.

"Babies were born and others aborted, old folks have died, a new war has started. There was sex and there was love, crimes were committed, people were fired, people retired, and others were hired. Someone ate some forbidden fruit, drinks were mixed, and a flat tire was fixed. Dreams were realized and dreams were dashed, the neighbors were cooking some corned beef hash. Someone put an eye out with that thing, bets were laid, little kids played. Some folks were cured and others endured, some rest assured. As for me, I hung your door trimmed out your closet, which seems insignificant in light of what's going on out there. Does that answer your question?"

My wife has high standards and will only accept my best. We often work together as a design and build team. She pushes me. She also believes in me, sometimes more than I've believed in myself. Sometimes a "do over" is requested on something I build.

Indignant, I proclaim, "You don't need a carpenter, you need a magician."

Or: "It can't be done, and I'm not gonna do it."

I've thought about putting that on my business card right under don't call this number. But when it's all said and done and I'm admiring the finished product, I can thank my wife for putting my feet to the fire. As I've said, she's smarter than I am. Thank God.

While in prison daydreaming about what my future life would look like once released, I couldn't have known I was thinking way too small. I couldn't imagine that I would experience abundance and joy, but here I am comfortable in my own skin. I'm even comfortable in my wife's skin. There's a lot of potential in prison—intelligent, artistic, funny people with very big addictions and very little common sense. When offered a new way to live, many would take to exercise or amino acids as a cure-all. Many who were released did look quite healthy but would end up back in, a shell of their former selves, beaten down once again by their poison of choice. For most of my life, I shared their mantra: "I am an island. Human interaction is overrated. I don't talk about my stuff," all the way to the gates of the prison. I have to be careful and not forget that there's a whole world of help out there at my fingertips for free.

Thank you for my life.

Chapter 73
Kid Stuff

While out on a walk with Zinc through our neighborhood I saw *The One*. It was looking through a time machine back to my knuckle-headed, glorious past.

When I was a kid, I took action to ensure that I would be entertained on a budget throughout my childhood. Sometimes this required dangerous and outrageous things that my mother never need know. She was well schooled at the art of ass whoopin. She learned that from my dad, whose only parenting style was hands on. As a result, she never knew about a lot of things. Like the rope swing that went seventy-five feet out over a ravine's canyon, until swinging came to an abrupt halt due to a pretty severe accident. I didn't mention to her the rock filled bottle fights (Mickey's Big Mouth bottles worked best) with metal garbage can lids for shields. I hid the bomb making and the making of human dummies with ketchup poured over them and deposited on the side of the road. And the incessant climbing of trees, not just any trees but majestic old growth trees as much as 100 feet up into the air. I imagine that those activities are all filed in the lamo-geezer archives in today's virtual kid world. A thing of the past, I figured until Zinc and I discovered the *One,* who is carrying the torch.

First, I noticed some serious digging going on. I thought, "Child labor, failed sewer line." A couple of days later I discovered it wasn't a ditch, but a giant mud hole disguised as a swimming pool with a trampoline set up next to it to practice cannonballs. I'm talking about a 15-foot by 15 feet wide and 8-foot deep mud puddle.

As a kid, I would have thought, "That guy's Dad is a hero."

As an adult I'm thinking, "Is he frickin' insane?"

My contractor's brain went on overload. I could envision the water from the mud hole percolating into the ground and undermining the foundation, not to mention the flooded basement, mold, etc.

But for father mud-hole, the love of his child was well worth it. I hail from uber-white trash. I completely get it; you make do with what you've got. I fully expect that boy to be very successful, landscape designer, basement weatherization professional or possible Olympic athlete. Whatever he chooses to do, after some extensive therapy, he will succeed.

I will too, I remind myself often, forever leaving the connections to dope and dye packs behind, grateful for the way instead I've been welcomed back to life.

Recently, I bought my wife a triple beam Ohaus scale on Craigslist. Just like the ones I used to use while weighing out my coke and weed when I was a young criminal. My wife is not a drug dealer. She uses the scale to weigh out her metal oxides and frit for tin glazes, a centuries-old method of glaze firing for her artwork. I purchased it from a grizzled old white geezer in the White Center neighborhood of West

Seattle. He had a yard full of crusty cars and a garage full of unrelated stuff, twenty or so drum sets and a multitude of other lost gadgets and gizmos that were all worth money.

Being a drummer, I asked him "Do you play?"

I got an emphatic and surly, "NO," like it was the stupidest question in the world.

I left with him calling after me "let me know if you need anything else."

"You mean besides my head examined?" I yelled over my shoulder.

I was sure that I had just purchased some stolen merchandise from a fence. While I made my escape, I watched for the ever-present blue lights in the rearview mirror aware of what neighborhood I had wandered back into, old memories of my time there flooded back.

Chapter 74
Life in the Black

The more time passes on, the more I sever the ties to my old life. Part of that was a long financial slog toward making amends. Restitution to the banks I robbed was part of the plea package that I accepted. After being indicted on eleven counts of unarmed bank robbery, I pled guilty to six, all Washington Mutuals. Try as I might, I couldn't single-handedly keep them afloat. Kerry Killinger must be disappointed in me.

I paid 50 percent of everything I made while locked up and set up a payment plan for the rest after my release. It took me a total of fourteen years to pay off that bank money and only about two months to put it in my arm. Bad career move and not recommended.

Restitution to my mother was to be the best son I could be and to make sure all her needs were met. I took great care of her for the last nine years of her life. She valued her independence and could only tolerate me piecemeal. Some things would never change.

In all of my movement forward, I came across the one part of moving from my old life that I did not welcome. My mother was never a complainer, even at eighty-six years old.

She experienced a wave of what I thought were age-related aches and pains. To get her to admit it and go to the doctor was like pulling teeth. She finally agreed. She was riddled with lung cancer. It had broken a rib and a vertebrae in her back. This was October 1.

My sisters and I sat with her in shifts around the clock. She wasn't afraid and never cried. She felt at eighty-six that it was a good run, especially for a fifty-seven year smoker. We cried like babies. When the oncologist started to discuss chemo, she waved her hand through the air, cut her off and said, "I'm not going through that. What's the point?"

She had a parade of visitors and comforted all of them.

"Don't worry about me, I'll be alright," she'd say.

"I've got a little money," she said. "You guys pay my bills and divvy up the rest."

She said it like it was no big deal. She lived small, so to close up shop didn't take much, two or three days at the most. She said it like she was going on a cruise. It made me feel like I was killing her.

Baseball was one of her passions. She knew a lot about the game, recited batting averages and on-base percentages. We talked about another crappy season completed by the Mariners and watched someone else play in the post season. We talked a bit about her family of origin. I learned things that I had never known.

"Great Aunt Tay was a lesbian," she proclaimed.

Who knew?

We did not talk about death but sat there thinking about it constantly.

I was grateful for the constant drip of morphine that took her pain away. We were told she could have all she wanted. I reflected on the constant drip of narcotics that had almost taken me away, glad to be off to a meeting later. She told me she was proud of me and loved me. We both knew how hard it was for her to say.

That was Thursday.

Watching her chest barely move up and down, I said goodbye to my sisters and planned to return for the Friday day shift before I headed out.

My sisters called me at 6:55 p.m., to say she was gone. Her riddled lungs had finally shut down.

After cremation, we split mom up in three urns. She has since lived in my basement next to the self-help books. This is as close as she'd ever gotten to recovery. She was always quiet, even more so now, but I can feel her presence. She's a little chunkier than I would have expected. I don't know if the oven got hot enough. I know she's not all there. I only have some of her, but I'm not sure what of her I do have. Hopefully, a little of everything. She's living with Pam and Vicki too unless they've already given her a proper send-off.

Mom was always frugal, didn't want the expense of a fancy funeral and didn't care about being fussed over, hence, the cremation. I'm thinking about taking her on a ferryboat ride To Whidbey Island where we once lived. She'd like that. So far I've been indecisive about a send off in Puget Sound because of the substantial possibility of ash blowback. I don't even know if she ever learned to swim, or if it matters. I'll ask around.

My wife is a ceramicist and a sculptor, I may ask her to create a small bust of my Mom from a portion of my portion before the send off, but I don't know if that would be morbid. It's nice to be able to offer sanctuary to my mom before she finds her final resting place. It's the least I could do.

Chapter 75
Raiders Revisited

I got a call from some of my old high school stoner friends to say they were attending our 35th reunion.

"You're missing a great party," I was told.

I was content with my party of two, Terrell and me in our home.

They happened to all still be single. I talked to Lenny, who claimed to be selling surplus black market Soviet military equipment in the Nevada desert and railing against the government. Back in the day he had hooked up my free power when I was an urban weed farmer. He's still an *off the grid* kind of guy. At thirteen, he was somewhat of a child genius. He played jazz piano and built his radio station broadcasting from his bedroom. He could tear down and rebuild any car. He worked on a dragster with super fat back tires in the back and what look like bicycle tires in the front. A funny car. Those cars are fueled with nitrous. It didn't take long before my friends and I filled our tanks with nitrous oxide. We would get big blue tanks and fill up hefty bags with a chunk of garden hose on the end, sit in what felt like a safe place, a beanbag chair, and huff. Blue lips were always a crowd pleaser. We stopped short of pulling out each other's teeth. Seatbelts should have been part of the gig because when I huffed nitrous oxide I had a tendency to get up and run into walls. Those weren't the good old days.

Grateful to have slowed down, I said thanks-but-no-thanks to the drugs and alcohol offered while reminiscing about the bad old days. I wouldn't trade what I've got for all the Kalashnikovs in Area 51.

I am constantly reminded by the chasm of my life now and then, and yet how both remain muddled within me. Like the time when, while I worked on a neighbor's house, right next door burglars broke into eighty-five-year-old Mrs. Burke's house while she took a nap. I heard another neighbor yell, and I gave chase with my framing hammer in hand. Later, after they were caught, I was informed by the police, that they were seventeen years old and packing heat. It's just like me to bring a hammer to a gunfight.

My view of money has changed too. The purpose of money is to support life. This is the conclusion Terrell and I came to when making the decision to have our dog Zinc's spleen removed. A massive cancerous tumor had caught a ride and was sucking the life out of our beloved Elkhound before our very eyes. He had lost his appetite as well as 20 percent of his body weight. It was heartbreaking. Zinc had become the ambassador for the Seattle Animal Shelter. His profound transformation from psychotic killer beast from the icy north to lovable Barney the dinosaur dog resulted in the rescue of many pets by our neighbors, or vice versa.

I was told there was an 80 percent chance that cancer would spread to the rest of Zinc. I felt I owed him a chance at life since he added so much to the enrichment of mine. I'd hate to think that someone would make the decision to put me down over a few bucks. After a biopsy, we discovered the cancer was contained in the tumor.

Despite a scar from stem to stern, it's like it never happened. He acts like the same ole dog. Zinc lives in the moment, something I've been trying to learn my whole life. I'm looking forward to my teacher being around for a long time.

After gnawing at his stitches, I had to take him back into the vet for a couple of staples. Emerging from the back, he announced his displeasure in front of a crowd in the waiting room by way of a massive dump he presented on the scale. How much did it weigh? That's my boy.

With my pal back home, I remembered a situation my friend was in. His dog Splash was hit by a car and needed a leg amputated in order to stay alive. He thought it best just to put Splash down. He told me he was concerned that the Splash's quality of life would be diminished while navigating on three legs. Eventually, he opted for amputation. When he brought the dog home, post-surgery, he was prepared to carry Splash up the stairs and into the house for his new life of doggie dependence. But, when the back of the S.U.V. was opened, Splash flew out and bounded up the stairs wagging his tail. It didn't seem to be a hardship at that moment. There would be no life of dependence, only love and exercise just like before.

Chapter 76
A Gentle Reminder

The oldest house in my neighborhood just went away. It was built as a hunting lodge for the rich folk of Mercer Island just across the water. It stood proud for 112 years and was knocked down in little more than a few sad hours only to be replaced by a gigantic ugly box. I'm sad about that. Any indication that it had ever existed is gone. That'll be how it is for me one day. Poof.

The house had belonged to Dianne, one block up and right around the corner. She was a little eccentric with her garish wardrobe, sloth style fingernails, and Tami Faye makeup, but a nice enough gal as far as I could tell. Before she left for work one day her husband had told her, "I left a couple of Tylenol on the counter for you, you're going to need them."

That was his parting gift.

Later, my wife and I heard what sounded like a serious catfight and were a little concerned for our beloved feline Clementine.

"That's a person," Terrell said.

Someone was shrieking hysterically, so we ran with purpose in that direction. There was a group of neighbors, slack-jawed gawkers, in the street, paralyzed into inactivity and too freaked out to cross the invisible line of death. We arrived just in time to see Larry, Dianne's husband of thirty years, on the ground with a rope around his neck. He stared straight up at us with his thickly veined blue face and bulged-out milky eyes. She had cut him down from the barren maple tree that looked as dead as he did. She looked as though she could have stabbed him with that knife for what he had just done to her. He had hit the rockery and from the unnatural look of his twisted body, I believe he had broken his back. He didn't feel a thing though, as he had been dead for the better part of the day. No one had even noticed him swinging from that tree.

We took Dianne away from the immediate area and comforted her to the best of our limited ability. A stopgap measure until the pros arrived. In Seattle, you can call 9-1-1 and say gunshots fired, and wait and wait, but a suicide nets immediate results. The complete death squad, which included coroner, medics, fire department and police arrived almost instantaneously. They sent us away saying, "Thanks for your help. We've got it from here."

Dianne's personal wrecking ball had knocked her clean off her foundation. This tragedy required her to move away and rebuild her life somewhere else.

Something shifted in me on that late March afternoon. I felt that I had been resting on my laurels. I clearly understood that my life is finite. I hadn't recently been a full participant or paid enough attention. The shiny newness of life after prison had slowly worn off, and I was in dangerous territory. I could no longer say, "I'll take care of that tomorrow." It took the death of Larry for me to address two areas of my life that I painfully pretended didn't need attention. I didn't want to be like Larry, alone inside my head and whistling in the dark.

I saw a guy do a header off of the upper running track and hit the gym floor twenty-five feet below while I was in prison, but I had no connection to him at all and it didn't affect me. It's the kind of thing I fully expected considering my circumstances. Those were the days I worked from the John Wayne handbook, not feeling in public.

I reflected long and hard on the notion of checking out when I was in my disease and never considered how incredibly selfish that would have been. This I got to see through Dianne's eyes. In a roundabout way, by taking his life, my neighbor added to the joy and abundance of mine. He carried his message right to his grave. I've heard it said in recovery that some must die so others can live. This was Larry's gift.

I saw Dianne for a couple of years after on her way to the bus stop to go to work. She had been in therapy for some time and she said that it helped. She did look as though she was doing better. She referred to me as her angel. What I know about my angels is that an act of kindness and a little compassion can go a long way on any day.

.

Chapter 77
Do Over

God gave me a reset button. I no longer have to lug around someone who's trying to kill me. "That's just the way it is" carries no more weight because there are alternatives. Everyday has meaning, and the joy of living is stronger than the desire to harm myself. People are no longer out to get me. My misery was of my own making. The gaping hole that existed within me has finally been filled, not with chemicals, but with love and the human experience. I open myself to abundance and H.P. delivers. Scary feelings are not something for me to run away from but to embrace. It is possible to stub my toe and not run off the rails. I now know how I'm going to make it through the day. I can dare to be ordinary, and I'll fit right in, many people are doing it. I'm worth more than a footnote in the neighborhood police blotter. There is enough room for me on this planet. I don't have to go try to find another one. These are some of the things I tell myself daily as I rocket through this short life that I've been gifted before I move on to the next.

About the Author

If Doug Piotter was a house, his Higher Power started the restoration project by taking him down to the studs. After two decades of reckless behavior, gripping drug addiction and petty crime evolving into bank robbery, Piotter's life became its own Ground Zero. The long hustle and life among the seedy addicts in Seattle ended on the day he started a 115-month prison sentence. But, the day of his arrest back in 1993 was also the last time he ever used drugs and the last time he ever committed a crime.

Piotter has built a successful construction company, sustaines a happy marriage to artist Terrell Lozada, is an active member of his recovery community and uncovered a hidden talent as a comedic author.

Doug is still alive in Seattle and aspires to go to Canada one day. He spends his time between running his construction business and being the world's best husband to his wife, artist Terrell Lozada. Being an avid talker, he shares his experiences with anyone who will listen, especially his dog Zinc.

For blogs, announcements and updates on future projects, visit dougpiotter.com.

CPSIA information can be obtained
at www.ICGtesting.com
Printed in the USA
FSOW04n1809030516
19981FS